CONTENTS

Published by Pedigree Books Ltd. Published 2011.

PEDIGREE BOOKS, BEECH HILL HOUSE,
WALNUT GARDENS, EXETER, DEVON EX4 4DH
shoot@pedigreegroup.co.uk

EDITOR COLIN MITCHELL
DESIGN STUART BIRTLES AND JONATHAN FINCH
THANKS TO: JON REEVES, RICHARD LEIGHTON AND BEN CRUMP

Pedigree®   **SHOOT**.CO.UK

HOT-SHOT HERNANDEZ!

Forget about double your money – Javier Hernandez is set to TRIPLE his earnings after a wonder start to his career in England.

Sir Alex Ferguson knew the Mexican was hot property when he bagged him on the eve of the 2010 World Cup finals.

But the Manchester United manager has admitted that even he was surprised at how quickly the striker fitted into the Premier League.

With 13 leagues goals and 20 in his first 45 appearances, it's fair to say that the £6m man was the best buy of 2010-11!

How did you settle in so quickly?
"People like Ryan Giggs, Paul Scholes and Rio Ferdinand help me and the other young players all the time. I have no problems being on the bench. I have understood that football is a team sport. It's not a game like golf or tennis. You have to help your team when you play from the beginning but also when you come on from the bench."

And what about Sir Alex Ferguson?
"I'm a Mexican playing at the best club in the world. Ferguson treats all of the players in the same way. He is a gentleman and he respects us. If Ferguson puts me on from the beginning that would be great, but if he doesn't that's ok too."

Did you dream the first year would be so good?
"Of course I imagined we would win the title but I never thought that I would play so often and score so many goals. I am delighted to be part of this great team. I want to win more titles with Manchester United. That first one was the most important one in my life so far."

How do you see yourself as a player?
"You will always see a player who exhausts himself on the pitch. Someone who is always running and knows there are good and bad matches, but someone who always hopes for good matches. I will never give up fighting and running."

And off the pitch?
"My family have made sure I've stayed down to earth. I don't feel bigger than anybody, despite my goals, success or medals. My friends have been with me through good and bad times."

What about the next campaign?
"I'm very motivated after a great first season with United. From now on I'll owe a great debt to Sir Alex for bringing me to Europe. My dream has not changed. I want to win many titles to give back to the team that opened the doors for me."

FACT FILE
JAVIER HERNANDEZ
Position: Striker
Height: 1.75m (5ft 9in)
Birth Date: June 1, 1988
Birth Place: Guadalajara, Mexico
Clubs: Chivas de Guadalajara, Manchester United
International: Mexico

DID YOU KNOW?
Manchester United scouts had been watching "Chicharito" Hernandez for nine months before he signed on July 1, 2010. Chief scout Jim Lawlor then compiled a big dossier on the player for Fergie who immediately decided to sign the striker.

There's no doubt that Javier Hernandez was one of the buys of the 2010-11 season. Here's are ten more signings who gave value for money...

1

DARREN BENT ASTON VILLA £24m from Sunderland

Many people were shocked at the club record fee Villa paid for Bent, but the clinical striker scored some crucial goals, including an impressive double against Arsenal. His seven goals helped keep the Villans away from relegation.

LUIS SUAREZ LIVERPOOL

£22m from Ajax

The Uruguay international scored four goals before the end of the season following his January move to Anfield. But it was his work rate and overall contribution that made him so impressive to Liverpool supporters. Great replacement for Fernando Torres.

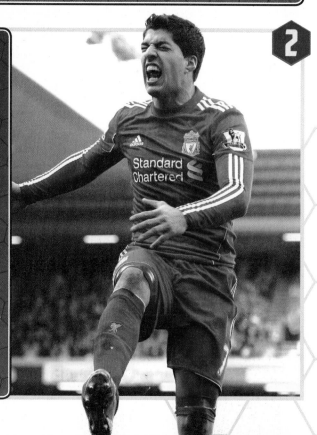

2

YAYA TOURE MANCHESTER CITY

£28m from Barcelona

Toure played defensively at Barcelona but since his arrival at Eastlands has enjoyed a more attacking role. This has seem him score some vital goals, including the one which won the FA Cup.

3

4

CHEIK TIOTE NEWCASTLE

£4m from Twente

Tiote enjoyed a brilliant first season in the Premier League and for many was Toon's Player of the Year. His superb volley against Arsenal in the 4-4 comeback was a highlight of his season. Needs to improve his disciplinary record.

5

RAUL MEIRELES
LIVERPOOL

£11.5m from Porto

With Mascherano gone, Aquilani on loan and Gerrard unfit, Meireles proved a more than able replacement. Five goals under Kenny Dalglish and Liverpool's Player of the Year.

6

JERMAINE PENNANT
STOKE

£3m from Zaragoza

Having returned to English football after a spell in Spain, Pennant finally delivered in the top-flight. His assured performances and assists helped Stoke reach Europe and the FA Cup Final.

7

ALI AL-HABSI
WIGAN ATHLETIC

Loan from Bolton

Wigan's Player of the Season, the Omani's amazing performances helped the Latics stay in the Premier League. He played 33 leagues games for Athletic – amazing when you consider he'd had just ten starts in his previous four years at Bolton.

8

RAFAEL VAN DER VAART TOTTENHAM

£8m from Real Madrid

The Dutchman scored goals and helped with assists. Van der Vaart was integral to Spurs' run in the Champions League and made the PFA Player of the Year shortlist.

BEN FOSTER
BIRMINGHAM CITY

£6m from Man United

It's not often a manager sells a player and then praises him – but that's just what Sir Alex Ferguson did with Foster. The Scot reckons the keeper should be England's No.1 and Foster did nothing to disprove that theory despite Birmingham being relegated.

9

10

PETER ODEMWINGIE
WEST BROM

£1m from Lokomotiv Moscow

Scored 15 Premier League goals in his first season of English football and was rewarded with a new contract at the Hawthorns. His goals helped the Baggies stay in the top-flight.

WORLD-BEATER!

HOW GARETH BALE BECAME PLAYERS' PLAYER OF THE YEAR

Gareth Bale is big. He's a big guy, a big name player and has a potential big money transfer fee! Yet just two years ago he was being written off as a teenager with talent who hadn't achieved his full potential.

Many pundits will tell you his amazing progress is thanks to the arrival at Tottenham of manager Harry Redknapp.

Welshman Bale will argue that he's just grown up and learned more about the game.

Both things are probably true. What is certainly correct is that during 2010-11, Gareth Bale played well enough to be named PFA Player of the Year by his fellow professionals.

It's an honour that has been presented since 1974 and one which every professional wants to win. To be the Players' Player means more than anything else.

"Obviously it is a massive honour to even be on the list for that trophy and only the fourth from Tottenham," admits Bale.

"It is massive and I want to build on this. I want to reach as high as I can. I think I have still got a lot to improve on but if I keep working hard then hopefully I can keep improving and getting better," he added.

Yet back in 2009-10 Bale appeared to be struggling and it looked like he might not make the breakthrough. He was undeterred.

"I have always believed in what I could do I just needed to be given a chance to play week-in week-out at Tottenham. There is no better way to learn," he admits.

"I don't feel the weight of expectation, I am never daunted. I take everything as just another game. Once you step onto the pitch you think about giving 100 per cent, not where you are or who you are.

"I have always believed in what I could do I just needed to be given a chance to play week-in week-out at Tottenham. There is no better way to learn,"

"I've always believed in myself but this has happened in such a short space of time, which is a bit strange. I kind of try and take it in my stride and just work hard on the football pitch."

Life at Spurs was indeed good for most of 2010-11 with Tottenham's incredible first attempt at the Champions League providing Bale with an amazing journey.

"I'm enjoying my football at Tottenham, we've got a great manager and a great young squad.

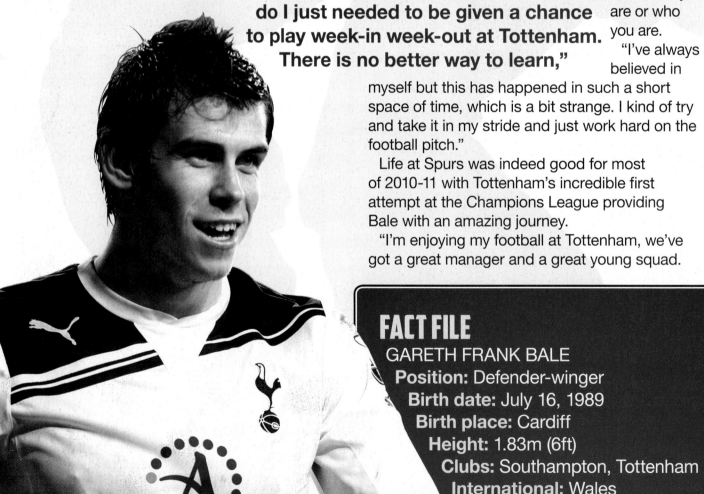

FACT FILE
GARETH FRANK BALE
Position: Defender-winger
Birth date: July 16, 1989
Birth place: Cardiff
Height: 1.83m (6ft)
Clubs: Southampton, Tottenham
International: Wales

SHOOT'S ULTIMATE BOOK OF FOOTBALL 2012

BALE IN NUMBERS

24 League games he appeared in without Tottenham getting a victory!

2 years after joining Spurs he took part in his first Premier League victory for them as an 85th minute substitute against Burnley.

7 Million pounds paid to Southampton to buy him in 2007.

50 Million pounds transfer fee put on his head by experts.

17 The age at which he joined Spurs.

26 of August 2007 when he made his Tottenham debut at Manchester United.

2008 The year boss Harry Redknapp arrived and starting developing Bale's talent.

3 other Tottenham players have been PFA Player of the Year – keeper Pat Jennings, striker Clive Allen and winger David Ginola.

5 The times the PFA award has been given to a Welshman. The other winners were Ian Rush, Mark Hughes (twice), Ryan Giggs.

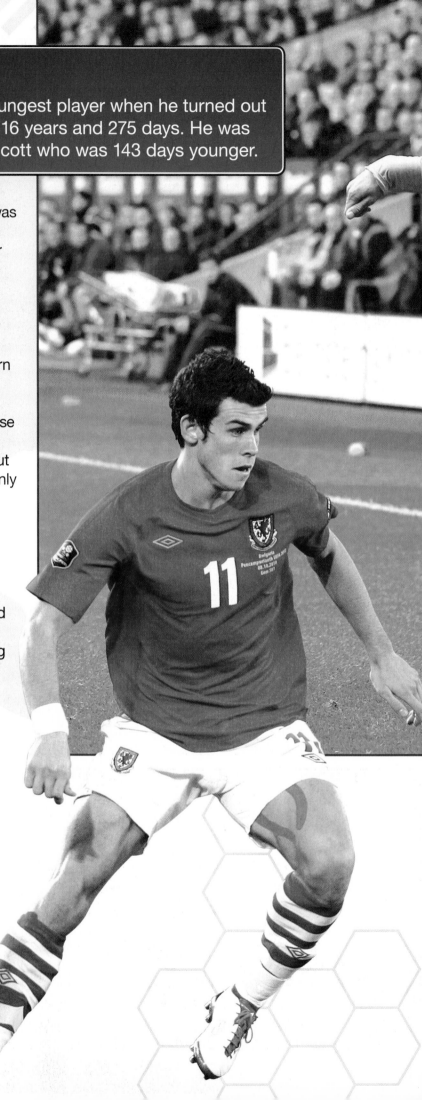

It's exciting times," he said.

"I suppose the hat-trick against Inter Milan was the highlight, and then beating them at home have been the top moments of that season for me. Hopefully there is more to come…

"It was a lot to ask us to do, both in the Premier League and the Champions League, I think we coped with it well."

Don't expect Bale to sit back and soak up the adulation – he knows he has much to learn and rubbishes talk of superstardom.

"I am still young, I am still learning but it you look at the likes of Messi and Ronaldo then those are the levels you have to aspire to," he admits.

"It's very nice if people say nice things about me but if you tell me I am a superstar I certainly don't think of myself that way. I am more concerned about what is to come, and I believe there is a lot more."

Looking back to when he was a teenager newly arrived in London, Bale reckons it just took him time to adapt and learn about life.

"I suppose I am tougher both physically and mentally but it is just a part of growing up. I was 17 when I joined Tottenham and moving to London at that age is difficult. You just grow up and mature naturally, so it was always just a matter of time. Now I hope it is showing on the pitch."

So what does he see as his strengths? "If I am one on one with someone I will fancy myself against whoever I am up against," he said. "I need to cope an adapt when they starting sticking two or three players on me, to go inside, go outside and mix things up with different runs."

"It's very nice if people say nice things about me but if you tell me I am a superstar I certainly don't think of myself that way. I am more concerned about what is to come and I believe there is a lot more."

WHAT HIS BOSS SAYS...

Tottenham boss **Harry Redknapp** reckons he wouldn't sell Gareth Bale for £100m – although he wouldn't get much say in the matter if Spurs got offered that type of cash! The experienced gaffer admits that his left-sided star is on course to become one of the world's best, and wants to hang on to him.

"Gareth has got better and better and has everything to become a world-class player," said Redknapp, who was responsible for bringing through a host of current stars during his time at West Ham.

Redknapp added: "He has pace, can dribble, shoot, head, he's got the lot. He still has plenty to learn and he will do that.

"It's now a question of whether he will become the world's best left back or best left-sided player. Both options are open to him."

Now check out all of the previous PFA Player of the Year winners **ON PAGE 14**

PFA PLAYERS' PLAYER OF THE YEAR

ROLL OF HONOUR

There's an impressive list of players who have lifted the PFA Player of the Year Award – starting with Leeds United's hardman Norman Hunter in 1973-74.
The first Premier League award went to Aston Villa defender Paul McGrath – but only two players have managed to retain the title for two seasons, Arsenal goal legend Thierry Henry and Manchester United's twinkle toed Cristiano Ronaldo.

THE EARLY YEARS 1974-1992

1974 Norman Hunter, Leeds United

1975 Colin Todd, Derby County

1976 Pat Jennings, Tottenham Hotspur

1977 Andy Gray, Aston Villa

1978 Peter Shilton, Nottingham Forest

1979 Liam Brady, Arsenal

1980 Terry McDermott, Liverpool

1981 John Wark, Ipswich Town

1982 Kevin Keegan, Southampton

1983 Kenny Dalglish, Liverpool

1984 Ian Rush, Liverpool

1985 Peter Reid, Everton

1986 Gary Lineker, Everton

1987 Clive Allen, Tottenham Hotspur

1988 John Barnes, Liverpool

1989 Mark Hughes, Manchester United

1990 David Platt, Aston Villa

1991 Mark Hughes, Manchester United

1992 Gary Pallister, Manchester United

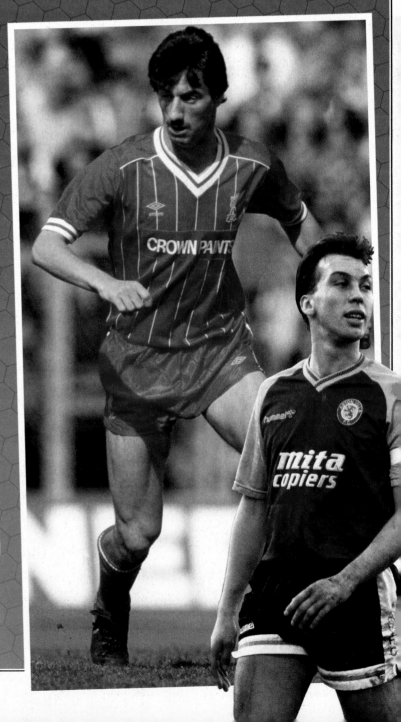

THE PREMIER LEAGUE YEARS

1993 Paul McGrath, Aston Villa

1994 Eric Cantona, Manchester United

1995 Alan Shearer, Blackburn Rovers

1996 Les Ferdinand, Newcastle United

1997 Alan Shearer, Newcastle United

1998 Dennis Bergkamp, Arsenal

1999 David Ginola, Tottenham Hotspur

2000 Roy Keane, Manchester United

2001 Teddy Sheringham, Manchester United

2002 Ruud van Nistelrooy, Manchester United

2003 Thierry Henry, Arsenal

2004 Thierry Henry, Arsenal

2005 John Terry, Chelsea

2006 Steven Gerrard, Liverpool

2007 Cristiano Ronaldo, Manchester United

2008 Cristiano Ronaldo, Manchester United

2009 Ryan Giggs, Manchester United

2010 Wayne Rooney, Manchester United

2011 Gareth Bale, Tottenham Hotspur

WHAT HAPPENED TO THEM?

What some of the former winners are doing now...

ANDY GRAY – working as a radio pundit

LIAM BRADY – coaching the rising stars of Arsenal

TERRY MCDERMOTT – assistant manager at Huddersfield

GARY LINEKER – BBC TV presenter

DAVID PLATT – coaching at Manchester City

ERIC CANTONA – starring in films

LES FERDINAND – coaching Tottenham's frontmen

TEDDY SHERINGHAM – professional poker expert!

THIERRY HENRY – scoring for New York Red Bulls

WE WERE THERE...

2001: The Ipswich Town changing room was a good place for Titus Bramble having just made his mark during a two-game loan to Colchester. The defender was being hailed as the 'next big thing' and *Shoot* was there to get his first major magazine interview. Quiet but confident, the local-born star was outlining his hopes for the future – which would take in a £6m move to Sir Bobby Robson's Newcastle before a transfer to Wigan and then back north to the Geordie's bitter rivals Sunderland. Among his team-mates at Portman Road before he left… Darren Bent, Darren Ambrose, Hermann Hreidarsson, Matt Holland and Jim Magilton.

WORLD-CLASS
STARS

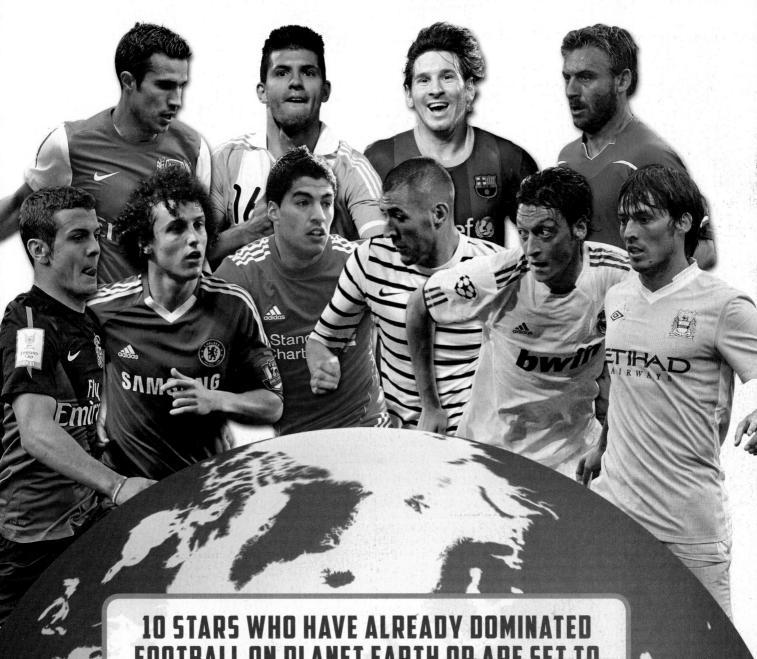

10 STARS WHO HAVE ALREADY DOMINATED FOOTBALL ON PLANET EARTH OR ARE SET TO MAKE THEIR MARK OVER THE COMING YEARS

MESSI

FACT FILE

LIONEL ANDRES MESSI
Position: Midfielder
Height: 1.69m (5ft 7in)
Birth Date: June 24, 1987
Birth Place:
Rosario, Argentina
Clubs: Barcelona
International:
Argentina

THEY SAY...

"Luckily we have the best player in the world. Messi is everything for the Seleccion, we will not find anyone better. He is a very important player to the group and they listen to him in all of the meetings."

SERGIO BATISTA
Argentina coach

"Messi is the best player in the world by a large distance. It is difficult because he's not always in the game, but when he gets on the ball he's really dangerous and unstoppable. When he changes direction at such pace no-one can stay with him. He is very young but he can achieve a lot. He has six or seven years in front of him and he can reach unbelievable levels."

ARSENE WENGER
Arsenal manager

THE MAGICIAN

World Player of the Year in both 2009 and 2010 – Lionel Messi is quite simply one of the top footballers on the planet.

He's not the tallest player but once he gets the ball at his feet he could quite easily be the most deadliest!

His second goal against Real Madrid in the first-leg of last season's Champions League semi-final was one of the best-ever in the competition and ranks with some of the leading goals ever scored.

The Argentina forward can play wide, in the middle or as an out and out striker. But so long as he is on the pitch he is a danger whatever position he occupies!

Messi can breeze past midfielders and defenders as it they aren't even there. He makes ball control look simple and his striking power is awesome.

He plays with a smile on his face, rarely gets into conflicts and just gets on with doing what we all want: entertaining fans with his amazing skills.

HE SAYS... "I know we can never be sure of what's going to happen in football, but I would never go to Real Madrid. My intention is to play in Barcelona my whole career. The team should always come first. If you only think about playing for yourself then you will go nowhere in football. Individual trophies are very nice to receive and I've been lucky enough to win several – but all of them were thanks to my team-mates."

LIONEL MESSI

ROBIN

THE HIGH FLYER

FACT FILE

ROBIN VAN PERSIE
Position: Striker
Height: 1.88m (6ft 2in)
Birth Date: August 6, 1983
Birth Place:
Rotterdam, Holland
Clubs:
Feyenoord, Arsenal
International:
Holland

THEY SAY...

"I've always been a fan of Robin's. I bought him at a time when not many people were convinced. He is a football fanatic. Every day of his life is focused on winning and being efficient. He is highly focused on doing well for the club. When you talk about youth, van Persie came here at the age of 21 and look at the way he has developed since his arrival."

ARSENE WENGER
Arsenal manager

"He is good on his right foot, even better on his left and decent in the air. Van Persie is a good finisher and scores goals galore."

Johan Cruyff *Holland legend*

Robin van Persie is the type of player who can change the outcome of the game with a turn of his speed or with a devastating shot on target.

The Dutch forward has averaged a goal every three games during his career – a fair return for any striker – but add his vital number of assists to the mix and it's easy to see why he is so important for club and country.

Arsenal without their Holland man are a much weaker prospect. Even his arrival from the bench gives the Gunners a massive lift.

Injuries have curtailed his career significantly and there is no doubt that had he been able to play more he would have lived up to the tag of "the new Dennis Bergkamp".

Like his fellow Holland international, van Persie has dribbling and shooting skills that can get fans on the edge of their seats.

His shooting from either side and from distance can be deadly effective and has twice made him Arsenal's top goal scorer and earned him their Player of the Season award in 2008-09.

HE SAYS... "I learned a lot from Bergkamp, not only in football but also in life. Football really became my profession and my whole life is organised to perform. In the past, I took it easier and had a bit of attitude. Now I approach it with my mind and heart. I try to advise younger players as I see they make the same mistakes during training or matches that I did in the past. Everyone needs to feel appreciated and that is something I missed during my younger years."

ROBIN VAN PERSIE

CITY'S SILVA LINING

FACT FILE

DAVID JOSUE JIMENEZ SILVA
Position: Midfielder
Height: 1.7m (5ft 7in)
Birth Date: January 8, 1986
Birth Place: Arguineguin, Spain
Clubs: Valencia, Eibar (loan), Celta Vigo (loan), Manchester City
International: Spain

THEY SAY...

"David Silva is the best signing we have made. He is the type of player who can win you the game. He can provide you with the sort of pass that puts you through one on one with the goalkeeper. He is one of the best players in the squad. He has freshened up the team and brought a new dimension to it."

CARLOS TEVEZ
Manchester City team-mate

"I think that David Silva is one of the best midfielders in Europe, and I hope he will be a very important player for us. I think he can make a big, big impact for Manchester City. He is a fantastic player."

ROBERTO MANCINI
Manchester City boss who bought Silva

David Silva was a highly rated and much-wanted player before his move to Manchester City in summer 2010.

Very few English fans probably realised just how good a player the Spaniard was before his £24m move from Valencia.

The attacking midfielder has proved to be the main link man when City move into an opponent's half, his incredible vision for the game allowing him to pick out precision passes to cut open rival defences.

Silva's quick feet make him a difficult customer to tackle and his

speed with the ball at his feet enables him to move out to the wing as well as run the centre of the park.

His first season at Eastlands saw him retain his place for almost every match – quite a feat at a club where a star-studded squad means team rotation is a regular event.

Three Player of the Month awards for the club in his first five months at City says everything about the immediate impact he made – and why Barcelona, Real Madrid and Chelsea had all been chasing his signature

Having made his international debut for Spain at the age of 20 he has since become a World Cup 2010 and Euro 2008 winner with the side.

HE SAYS... "I believe the Premier League is one of the best competitions in the world and I want to bring success to City and win trophies for them. City were the club that showed the most interest in me. They stuck their neck out and showed the more serious interest, that's why I went for it."

SHOOT'S ULTIMATE BOOK OF FOOTBALL 2012

DAVID SILVA

LAID BACK LUIZ

FACT FILE

DAVID LUIZ MOREIRA MARINHO

Position: Defender
Height: 1.85m (6ft 1in)
Birth Date: April 22, 1987
Birth Place:
Sao Paulo, Brazil
Clubs:
Vitoria, Benfica, Chelsea
International:
Brazil

THEY SAY...

"He's brilliant. It shows why Chelsea bought him, he really is a great addition to the squad."

PETR CECH *Chelsea keeper*

"He's incredible. He can play in midfield, he can play at right-back, he can play at left-back as well. He is very confident and assured of himself."

JOHN TERRY *Chelsea captain*

David Luiz looks so calm on the ball he's almost laidback!

But don't let that appearance fool you. Chelsea's Brazil defender is top drawer.

He makes tough defensive duties look simple and only breaks into a sweat when he has some extra-difficult duties to deal with!

The curly haired one is silky smooth when it comes to intercepting opposition forwards, cutting out deadly balls and dealing with defensive slip-ups made by team-mates.

His arrival in the Premier League in January 2011 was overshadowed by the £50m move of Fernando Torres to Stamford Bridge.

But it was Luiz who was quick to make a mark and impress the Blues' faithful. Supporters and team-mates were well-impressed at how quickly he settled into his new job.

And when they started calling him John Terry's eventual replacement you just knew he had arrived. Anyone who could even attempt to pull on JT's boots at the Bridge has to be a bit special.

HE SAYS... "I don't kick people. I just think football is a sport for men and we need to overcome our rivals as long as we keep it within the rules. It is a surprise to me that fans of other clubs have praised my game and goals. That signifies I am having success with Chelsea. But I am here to improve and to work with my new club, and not for individual success."

DAVID LUIZ

JACK WILSHERE

WONDERFUL WILSHERE

Jack Wilshere has the hopes of a nation resting on his shoulders – but it's a burden he looks well capable of carrying despite being just 19-years-old.

As he was coming through the ranks at Arsenal the midfielder was building up a formidable reputation as a rising star. Indeed, Gunners boss Arsene Wenger, one who is often reluctant to big-up youngsters too much, was quick to praise the young star.

Having come through the England youth ranks from the age of 14 – when he played for the Under-16s – Wilshere broke through to the Under-21s when he was still 17 and reached the full England side at the age of 18!

England's tenth-youngest player ever made his full international debut in 2010 and looked comfortable. His appearances since show just why he was on the edge of being named in the Three Lions World Cup squad for South Africa and why he was the 2011 PFA Young Player of the Year. Arsenal's youngest-ever player at the age of just 16 years and 256 days, Wilshere can operate anywhere in midfield. He can defend, attack and create which makes him a massive asset to any side.

HE SAYS... "In ten years I still want to be at Arsenal, winning trophies for my club and for the national team. My dad was great to me when I was growing up, he sacrificed a lot for me, finishing work early to take me training. He normally drives me home, we talk about the game afterwards in the car and he tells me if I've done well or if I haven't done so well."

FACT FILE

JACK ANDREW GARRY WILSHERE
Position: Midfielder
Height: 1.73m (5ft 8in)
Birth Date: January 1, 1992
Birth Place: Stevenage, Hertfordshire
Clubs: Arsenal, Bolton (loan)
International: England

THEY SAY...

"He can play any position in midfield because he is tactically intelligent. Jack is focused, he wants the ball and he wants to play. Jack is a generous player and gives you everything in every game. He always wants to play and that is good."

ARSENE WENGER
Arsenal manager

"The amount of good games Jack has played is special. I have never seen anyone who is 19 and that good in his role. He plays very mature – when you get older, you have the experience and know how to play each game, and sometimes I feel he has that already."

ROBIN VAN PERSIE
Arsenal team-mate

ITALIA

DANIELE DE ROSSI

ROCKIN' DE ROSSI

Dedicated to Roma from his childhood days, Daniele De Rossi is expected to leave his native Italy for a bigger team.

With the likes of Real Madrid and Manchester United having eyed up his midfield talents in recent years, it's obvious that he has undoubted quality.

A World Cup-winner with Italy, De Rossi has made more than 350 club appearances and turned out in excess of 60 times for his country.

His reputation is as an all-round battling midfielder, someone who can defend and control a game. He is not noted for his passing and isn't a prolific goal-scorer – but is one of those players who can dictate how a game is played.

Consistency is a vital part of his game as is his honest, hard-working dedication to his job.

Combative and with a number of cards to his name, De Rossi isn't a dirty player and is rated by his fellow professionals as being one of the fairest competitors around.

Nicknamed Captain Future, he was Italy's Young Player of the Year in 2006 and Player of the Year in 2009.

HE SAYS... "I like the manly game but I also like playing the ball around. I don't like it when the game gets too physical, not because I'm afraid but because I like the beautiful game. I work hard to become always a stronger player even at international level."

FACT FILE

DANIELE DE ROSSI
Position: Midfielder
Height: July 24, 1983
Birth Date: 1.84m (6ft)
Birth Place: Rome, Italy
Clubs: Roma
International: Italy

THEY SAY...

"Daniele De Rossi is a great champion. He's not just a player who has outstanding qualities and technical excellence, but he has human qualities and high moral standard."
GIAN PAOLO MONTALI
Roma director

"Daniele is one of the best midfielders in the world. I love the commitment Daniele has always made and will always make for the national team."
MARCELLO LIPPI
former Italy manager

KARIM BENZEMA

BRAVO BENZEMA!

With an average of almost a goal every other game, it's not difficult to see why a number of the world's top clubs have kept a close eye on Karim Benzema.

The France striker won four consecutive Ligue 1 titles with Lyon before he was bought by Real Madrid in summer 2009 for a fee of £35m.

Accused of not working hard enough when he first arrived in Spain, the forward accepted a kick up the backside from coach Jose Mourinho and returned to his glittering best.

His first year at the Bernabeu was so difficult that he missed out on his country's World Cup squad.

Manchester United boss Sir Alex Ferguson has been a long-time admirer of Benzema, whose family roots are in northern Algeria.

The striker has tremendous strength, lots of skills on the ball, a great strike and a few tricks to fool the smartest of defenders.

Deadly inside the box, he also has the ability to track back and turn defence into attack by holding up the ball or moving forwards with it.

HE SAYS... "I did not sign for Madrid to sign for another club soon after. I want to succeed here. Thanks to Mourinho I want to score and I want to run more. I feel much better than before. Mourinho is a great coach. He has managed to change my mentality. Now I'm a fighter."

FACT FILE

KARIM BENZEMA
Position: Striker
Height: December 19, 1987
Birth Date: 1.84m (6ft)
Birth Place: Lyon, France
Clubs: Lyon, Real Madrid
International: France

THEY SAY...

"Benzema must understand that he is extremely talented but that in itself is not enough. I need Karim. For me he is a very important player but he has to put himself out there. We need a striker who is sparky not one that is listless. Benzema is happy and we are happy with him."

JOSE MOURINHO
Real Madrid coach

"Karim's working very well and it was difficult to see him go through these tough times. Things were not going well for him, but he has now shown a good response."

CRISTIANO RONALDO
Madrid team-mate

MESUT OZIL

THERE'S ONLY ONE OZIL...

Great ball control, great vision and a wicked long-range shot – it's hard to criticise Mesut Ozil for not tracking back to do his defensive duties!

The German-born midfielder of Turkish descent has already been called his country's Zidane or Messi, high praise indeed and a tag which he is still trying to live up to.

A star at World Cup 2010, he earned a £12m move to Spanish giants Real Madrid and soon fitted in to their style of play. That fee now looks like a real bargain.

Local media – always a harsh critic in Spain – were full of praise for the young player's first season in their country, a sure sign that he had produced the goods.

Having progressed through his country's youth ranks Ozil made his full Germany debut at the age of 20 and he played in all of their games at South Africa 2010.

Ozil is an attacking team's dream with his ability to always move forwards. He never appears to go sideways or play the ball back and is always looking to create or score.

Although he is primarily left footed you can expect the ball to be fired off in the best direction possible for his team when he makes a pass.

HE SAYS... "I am already playing for the best and most famous club in the world. I'm proud to have got this far in my career, but I also know it's only the beginning. I don't need to be told I'm a long way from being complete in my football development, I have to keep learning and pushing myself. There will be no hiding place for me at Real and this is part of the challenge."

FACT FILE
MESUT OZIL
Position: Midfielder
Height: October 15, 1988
Birth Date: 1.81m (5ft 11in)
Birth Place: Gelsenkirchen, Germany
Clubs: Schalke, Werder Bremen, Real Madrid
International: Germany

THEY SAY...
"We do not want to put too much pressure on one player, but he has the ability to achieve anything. We in Germany are prone to rave about foreign players. We praise Wayne Rooney to the heavens, likewise [Cristiano] Ronaldo or Messi. But we have our own Messi. Our Messi is Ozil."

HORST HRUBESCH
Germany youth coach

"He's a player who can play for Real Madrid for ten years. His contract was running out so we could get him at a lot less than his actual market value. We really could not let a player of his quality escape from us, in these conditions."

JOSE MOURINHO
coach who bought him for Real Madrid

SERGIO AGUERO

SUPER SERGIO!

When you have broken a record set by the great Diego Maradona the only way for your career has to be up!

Sergio Aguero was just 35 days passed his 15th birthday when he made his debut in Argentina's top-flight, which beat the best set by Maradona who was ten days off his 16th birthday.

The links to the legend don't stop there – Aguero is married to Maradona's youngest daughter!

His record of 23 goals in just 54 league games for Independiente meant he was soon on the radars of European scouts and just a few weeks before his 18th birthday he signed for Atletico Madrid for a club record £20m.

Constantly linked with a move to the Premier League, Aguero was subject of a Juventus bid last summer but it was Manchester City's £38m offer than took him to the Etihad Stadium.

FIFA's Young Player of the Year in 2007 is an out and out striker with deadly speed, a lethal shot and a hard work ethic and strength. Unlike some of City's other expensive imports from overseas, Aguero said he would have no problems settling into his new home.

HE SAYS... "Once you get into the national team, everybody is on the same level. That's a very positive thing because nobody carries responsibility for the whole team on their shoulders. I always watched the Premier League on TV and I think it is the best league in the world, along with the Spanish league."

FACT FILE

SERGIO LEONEL AGUERO DEL CASTILLO
Position: Striker
Height: June 2, 1988
Birth Date: 1.75m (5ft 9in)
Birth Place: Quilmes, Argentina
Clubs: Independiente, Atletico Madrid, Man City
International: Argentina

THEY SAY...

"Sergio is a top player and he is only a young boy. He's scored lots of goals and I expect him to score a lot for us. He needs to get to know the Premier League because it's so different to La Liga."

ROBERTO MANCINI
Manchester City manager

"He looks like me when I was a player. He is strong, with thick legs. I took notice of that when I was in Spain. He uses his body a lot to shield the ball."

DIEGO MARADONA
Argentina legend

LUIS SUAREZ

SUAVE SUAREZ

When you are handed the famed No.7 shirt at Liverpool there's a lot to live up to.

Previously worn by the likes of Keegan, Beardsley and Dalglish it takes a big player to pull on the jersey.

Luis Suarez proved in a matter of weeks that he too could add his name with pride to that legendary shirt.

Forget the theory that overseas players take time to settle in English football. Suarez was ripping into defences from day one and had a "danger" label stuck on him almost immediately. Although the £23m buy from Ajax can play wide it's as a striker that he's at his most dangerous.

Running at defenders, creating chances from incredible angles and firing off shots at any opportunity, the Uruguayan is the type of player than any side would love to sign.

A former Holland Footballer of the Year, Suarez had been on the shopping list of a number of big clubs – but it was Liverpool's Kenny Dalglish who made the plunge for the Uruguay frontman who hit three goals in six appearances at World Cup 2010 – but missed the semi-final defeat to Holland because of suspension following a red card.

HE SAYS... "My aim is to work, to show the fans how hard I am ready to work. This league is completely different, it is a big league and has its own way of doing things. You have to be able to adapt to the way the game is played, have to be physical and strong. I have trouble understanding the Scouse accent – although Carra isn't too bad!"

LUIS ALBERTO SUAREZ DIAZ
Position: Striker
Height: 1.81m (5ft 11in)
Birth Date: January 24, 1987
Birth Place: Salto, Uruguay
Clubs: Nacional, Groningen, Ajax, Liverpool
International: Uruguay

THEY SAY...

"There are few players to come from abroad and settle like he has done. We speak in Dutch together on the pitch. But Luis's English is not bad either and that has helped him settle quickly. Although we are different players and offer different skills to the team, we are also both hard workers."

DIRK KUYT
Liverpool and Holland forward

"He just enjoys playing football. His style is very pleasing on the eye and his ability is fantastic. He gets as much joy out of someone else scoring as he does his own goals. We said when he came that we were pleased to have him and that he'd be a real asset - and he's proved that."

KENNY DALGLISH
Liverpool manager

END OF AN ERA

ENGLISH FOOTBALL SAID GOODBYE TO SOME LONG-SERVING PLAYERS LAST SEASON. SHOOT PAYS TRIBUTE...

EDWIN THE GREAT

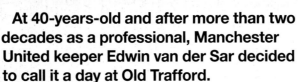

At 40-years-old and after more than two decades as a professional, Manchester United keeper Edwin van der Sar decided to call it a day at Old Trafford.

He called time on a glittering, trophy-laden career that saw him carve out a reputation as one of the best shot-stoppers of his generation.

The Holland star began his career at Ajax and soon established himself in the first-team, playing regularly in domestic and European competition for the Amsterdam giants.

After four league titles as part of the famous Ajax team of the early-1990s that also included, Edgar Davids, Clarence Seedorf and Patrick Kluivert, van der Sar played a major role as the team won the 1995 European Cup, defeating AC Milan 1-0 in the final.

After nine years in Holland a move to Juventus beckoned in 1999, but van der Sar's spell as No.1 was short-lived as the Turin club splashed the cash on Italian stopper, Gianluigi Buffon, meaning the Dutchman spent just two seasons in Serie A.

The service to his country was also excellent.

WHAT HIS BOSS SAYS...

"Fantastic - a magnificent person, professional goalkeeper, an absolute marvellous career he's had. He's an example to anyone who wants to become a keeper. Edwin sails through life without any changes. He has a consistent nature. He's unflappable. He's calm, he doesn't look to search for press for himself, he's happy with what he's achieved in life and he's not searching for anything, he's such a good man. There will always be comparisons between Peter Schmeichel and Edwin - in my time they've been the two outstanding goalkeepers, not just here but in football."
Sir Alex Ferguson *United boss*

FACT FILE

Position: Keeper
Birth Date:
October 29, 1970
Birth Place:
Voorhout, Holland
Clubs: Ajax, Juventus,
Fulham, Manchester United
International:
Holland (130 caps, 0 goals)
Honours:
Champions League 1995,
2008; UEFA Cup 1992;
European Super Cup 1995;
World Club Cup 2008;
Intercontinental Cup 1995;
Dutch Eredivisie 1994,
1995, 1996, 1998; Dutch
Cup 1993, 1998, 1999;
Premier League: 2007,
2008, 2009, 2011
League Cup: 2006

After making his Holland debut in 1995 he went on to be capped a record 130 times by the Oranje.

He went to seven major tournaments, including three World Cups, and came closest to international success in Euro 2000 as the Dutch were knocked out by Italy in the semi-finals on penalties.

After a slightly disappointing spell in Italy with Juventus, he signed for Premier League newcomers Fulham in 2001 and played an important role as the West London club established themselves in the top-flight.

After four years with the Cottagers, van der Sar returned to the big time with a move to Manchester United in 2005.

His United career will be remembered for the crucial match-winning penalty save in the 2008 European Champions League Final, but Reds fans saw him as the man to finally replace the almost irreplaceable Peter Schmeichel between the sticks.

After three seasons without a league title, United reclaimed their crown in 2007 with van der Sar's reliability and marshalling of his defence a crucial factor in the team's success.

Cool and calm with the ball at his feet, van der Sar's distribution is one of his major strengths and United have certainly benefited from that.

His quick and powerful throws set many counter-attacks in motion and his ability to control, pass and clear the ball with either foot helped get the Red Devils out of tight situations and maintain their free-flowing passing approach.

VAN DER SAR ON RETIREMENT...

"It is now time to pay attention to my family. Do not ask me how or why, but suddenly you know. My age played no role. I am 40-years, but I still feel fit. It's nice to be appreciated but the main thing is to win prizes. It's all about enjoying myself and winning those prizes. I gave up the international team so I could focus all my energy and attention on United. I think that every year when you play for a club like United you want to be champions and do well in the Champions League."

WHAT THEY SAY ABOUT HIM...

"I saw him when he was still playing for Ajax in the Champions League Final. At that time he was a great example when the new rule came in that the goalkeeper cannot pick up back passes. Everybody could see that he was playing well with both feet and they were using him a lot. He showed that in the future everyone should develop their kicking."

Petr Cech, *Chelsea and Czech Republic keeper*

"I think Edwin has done tremendously well. It was great to see him give stability to the team. You could see the faith and trust everyone had in him. He is an inspiration to the players in front of him."

Peter Schmeichel
United's legendary keeper

END OF AN ERA CONTINUES WITH A SHOOT TRIBUTE TO **GARY NEVILLE** ON PAGE 40

GOODBYE RED NEV

When Gary Neville announced his retirement in the middle of a season, it caught many fans by surprise, but those who know the character of the man, knew that the announcement was never going to be too far away.

Once he stopped being a useful part of the squad, who could make a difference on the pitch, Neville knew it would be time to hang up his boots.

After a couple of below-par performances against West Brom and Stoke City, Gary realised he had become a 'passenger' and it was time to step off the Man United juggernaut.

A staunch United fan, Neville lived his dream to represent the club he loved for the whole of his playing career.

After breaking through the ranks as one of Fergie's Fledglings, alongside the likes of David Beckham, Nicky Butt, Paul Scholes and his younger brother Phil, Gary became United's first choice right-back, a position he retained for almost 15 years.

Red Nev, as he was nicknamed, not just because of his affinity with United, but for his

WHAT HIS BOSS SAYS ...

"Gary was the best English right-back of his generation. He is an example to any young professional; hard-working, loyal and intelligent. His fantastic career at Old Trafford has cemented his place in the affection of the club's supporters everywhere. He came to us as a 13-year-old boy, an avid United fan and remained that way all his life and made a great career out of a fantastic will and determination to be the best. He is an absolute legend at our club and will remain so for the rest of his life."

Sir Alex Ferguson *United boss*

FACT FILE

Position: Defender
Birth Date:
February 18, 1975
Birth Place:
Bury, Lancashire
Clubs: Manchester United
International:
England (85 caps, 0 goals)
Honours:
World Club Cup 2008;
Intercontinental Cup 1999;
Premier League 1996,
1997, 1999, 2000, 2001,
2003, 2007, 2009;
FA Cup 1996, 1999, 2004;
League Cup 2006, 2010.

outspoken views on the game, made his debut for the Red Devils in 1992, eventually succeeding Paul Parker at full-back in 1995.

A constant stream of honours followed as Neville claimed eight Premier League titles and was a major part of the 1999 Treble-winning side, forming a fantastic understanding with best-friend, Beckham, down United's right-flank.

He was also an England regular and made the Three Lions' right-back spot his own for more than a decade, performing admirably at three European Championships and two World Cups.

Neville gave heroic displays in memorable England performances against Holland at Euro '96, Argentina at the 1998 World Cup and that famous 5-1 win over Germany in 2001.

He had natural defensive talents, great timing in the tackle, bravery both challenging for the ball and in possession, and the pace over short distances to close down opponents and mark some of the best players out of games.

Neville was good going forward, his overlapping runs allowing wingers to use him as a decoy and whip in crosses, or creating space for himself to put in telling deliveries of his own. His long throws were a formidable attacking weapon and his range of passing was often underrated.

When Roy Keane left the club in 2005, Neville was made captain, an honour he relished. His passion for United was as obvious as his hatred for their rivals.

His badge-kissing celebration after United scored a last-minute winner against bitter rivals Liverpool will live long in the memory, but unlike many footballers who kiss different club badges with promiscuity, he meant it!

NEVILLE ON RETIREMENT...

"I have been a Manchester United fan all my life and fulfilled every dream I've ever had. There are so many people I want to thank and of course top of that list is Sir Alex Ferguson. He has given me so many opportunities and countless support over the last 20 years. He is truly one of the greatest managers. I relied upon qualities that weren't technical or skilful to get to where I did. I like to think there was a level of intelligence and physically I felt like I could run all day. Mentally I had to do whatever it took to win a game for Manchester United. Once you know it is not quite right you don't want to be a passenger."

WHAT THEY SAY ABOUT HIM...

"The best right-back in Premier League history, fact. He's going to be a big loss to our dressing room. Nev is loyal, funny, dedicated and talented.... a true Man United legend. He gave his all for the club he supported and won a load of medals."

Rio Ferdinand
Man United team-mate

"He had a wonderful hunger and desire to succeed, which kept him where he was in the game. A Manchester United icon."

Steve Bruce
Ex-Man United defender

END OF AN ERA CONTINUES WITH A SHOOT TRIBUTE TO **PAUL SCHOLES** ON PAGE 42

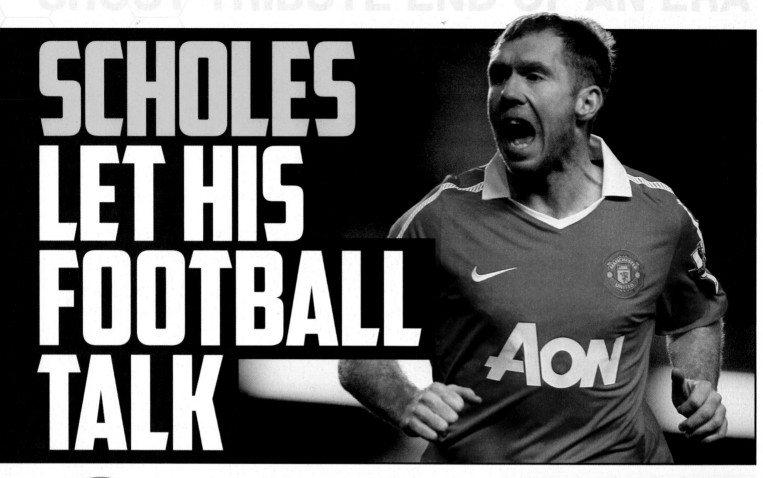

SCHOLES LET HIS FOOTBALL TALK

Off the pitch, Paul Scholes was the quiet man of football. He'd train or play the game and then go home to his family.

On the pitch he was a true Red Devil. Manchester United through and through he put his foot in where it hurts, battled as if his life depended on the outcome of the game, sprayed killer passes and scored amazing goals.

Whilst former team-mates like Beckham and Rooney hit the headlines on both the front and back pages, Scholesey was the man who wanted to shun the spotlight.

No racing to give interviews – quite the opposite – and no glitzy parties or paparazzi shots with celebrity friends.

"I only do what I have to and I won't go looking for interviews," Scholes told Shoot almost a decade ago when he met up with us to promote new boots for Nike.

So what did he make of all the fuss around his mate Beckham? "I think he gets all this stuff because of the player he is," said Scholes.

"If you are as good as David then you are bound to be in demand. He's a high profile person and a lot comes his way."

So how did the former England midfielder cope on those rare occasions when things didn't go to plan for Manchester United?

WHAT THEY SAY ABOUT HIM...

"What more can I say about Paul Scholes that I haven't said before. We are going to miss a truly unbelievable player. Paul has always been fully committed to this club and an inspiration to players of all ages."
Sir Alex Ferguson *United boss*

"He will be missed greatly. He is definitely the best player I have played with. I tried to ask him what he was doing but you don't get much out of him. Everyone will be sad to see him stop."
Wayne Rooney, *Manchester United and England*

Position: Midfielder
Birth Date:
November 16, 1974
Birth Place:
Salford, Manchester
Clubs: Manchester United
International:
England (66 caps, 14 goals)
Honours:
Premier League: 1996, 1997, 1999, 2000, 2001, 2003, 2007, 2008, 2009, 2011
FA Cup: 1996, 1999, 2004
League Cup: 2009, 2010
Champions League: 1999, 2008
Community Shield: 1996, 1997, 2003, 2008, 2010
World Club Cup: 1999
Intercontinental Cup: 1999

"You've just got to get on with it and not listen to what people say. You've got to bounce back from bad performances and there is no better way than going out and winning.

"The players know what they have to do within themselves. You can't be at Man United if you are not motivated or desperate to play well."

Like Beckham, Giggs and the Neville brothers, Scholes came through the ranks at Old Trafford. Even when he announced his decision to hang up his boots at the end of 2010-11 season, he remained part of the furniture by moving into a coaching role with the club.

Having won ten Premier League titles, two FA Cups and two European Cups, and a host of other silverware, he is one of United's most decorated players ever.

Back in 2001 there was even talk that Sir Alex Ferguson, the man who guided Scholes' career, could be retiring. Of course that just didn't happen and the silverware kept on flowing.

"You can't understate the impact he's had on a lot of the lads' careers. He gave us our chance and stuck with us. We all owe him such a lot," admitted Scholes.

Part of the FA Youth Cup-winning side of 1992, it wasn't until 1995 that Scholes staked his claim to a first-team berth.

Playing as a striker he scored nine goals in his first 12 games, then had to make way for Eric Cantona, returning from a ban. Two years later, and converted to an attacking midfield role, Scholes was established as a first choice on the team sheet.

In 2001 he told Shoot: "If I stay here for the rest of my career, then great – it's just up to me to keep playing well and deserve my place in the squad. I certainly haven't thought about leaving!"

He never did leave United, although he did call it a day with England in 2004. Having made his international debut in 1997, he became a mainstay for the Three Lions, although he had the dubious record of being the only England player sent off at the old Wembley.

His international appearances declined under Sven Goran Eriksson and he announced his retirement to concentrate on his club career.

Both Steve McClaren and Fabio Capello tried to lure the player back into the fold during their time in the England hot seat. Both failed.

SCHOLES ON RETIREMENT...

"I am not a man of many words but I can honestly say that playing football is all I have ever wanted to do and to have had such a long and successful career at Manchester United has been a real honour. This was not a decision that I have taken lightly but I feel now is the right time for me to stop playing. To have been part of the team that helped the club reach that 19th title is a great privilege."

WHAT THEY SAY ABOUT HIM...

"On the practice field, and in the locker room, he got his job done and went home to his family and that has always been the case with him. But if he was on the field, he gave 100 per cent."

Nicky Butt, *former United team-mate*

END OF AN ERA CONTINUES WITH A SHOOT TRIBUTE TO **PAUL DICKOV** ON PAGE 44

WANDERING STAR

Four hundred and eight career games and 118 goals for 11 clubs means that Paul Dickov left memories with a lot of fans before hanging up his boots.

Probably best remembered for his six years with Manchester City, the Scotland striker decided to call it a day so that he could concentrate on being manager of Oldham Athletic. His goals ratio wasn't top-class, but the former Arsenal trainee brought a lot more to all of his teams – not least his battling qualities that meant he was a constant pain in the side of defenders.

Dickov joined Manchester City from Arsenal in 1996 for around £1m and was to turn out for the team as they rose from the third tier of the English game to the Premier League.

Having suffered relegation to the third tier with City, Dickov produced some of the vital goals that helped them rise to the second-flight.

Injury restricted his appearances as the team battled for a place in the Premier League but he

WHAT THEY SAY ABOUT HIM...

"You can never question his enthusiasm for the game, he's had that throughout his career, but one thing that he's never had is putting goals to that enthusiasm. He put 20 goals on the board for us [2002-03] and once you have got a centre forward scoring goals you do not want to lose him."

Micky Adams
his boss at Leicester City

"I've known Paul a long time and he was with me at Blackpool. His experience is phenomenal and he's a fiery little so-and-so. He brings experience both on the pitch and in and around the dressing room.

Simon Grayson, *his boss at Blackpool and Leeds United*

FACT FILE

Position: Striker
Birth Date:
November 1, 1972
Birth Place:
Livingstone, Scotland
Clubs: Arsenal, Luton
(loan), Brighton (loan),
Manchester City (2),
Leicester City (2),
Blackburn, Crystal Palace
(loan), Blackpool (loan),
Derby (loan), Leeds United,
Oldham Athletic
International:
Scotland (10 caps, 1 goals)
Honours:
Arsenal (European Cup
Winners Cup); Man City
(Division two play-off final
win, Division One
promotion); League One
title (Leicester); Promotion
(Leeds and Leicester)

scored their third goal in the 4-1 victory over Blackburn Rovers – who he would later join – as promotion was sealed.

Dickov couldn't get regular football when the side was again relegated and made two moves – to Leicester City and then Blackburn – before rejoining City in 2006 for a second ill-fated spell which was hit by injuries.

He made four appearances for Leeds during a two-month spell early in 2010 but left after they were promoted to the Championship.

In summer that year he became player-manager of Oldham but restricted his league outings to just two games – the final one as a sub for the last 13 minutes of the season.

DICKOV ON RETIREMENT...

"I need to concentrate all my efforts on the management side. I am loving every minute of my new job and hope to have an equally long career. The ability to battle is one of the main parts of my game. I know my limits. I am not the sort who gets the ball and is then going to beat five or six players. Whether I'm playing well or not, the one thing you will get from me is 110 per cent."

WHAT HIS BOSS SAYS...

"To be fair to Dickov he gets the very best out of himself. The phrase 'to chase a piece of paper' could have been invented for him. He's hassling and harrying all over the place. Good luck to him, he deserves everything he gets out of the game."

Kevin Keegan
former Man City manager

END OF AN ERA CONTINUES WITH A SHOOT TRIBUTE TO **PATRICK VIEIRA** ON PAGE 46

CAPTAIN INVINCIBLE

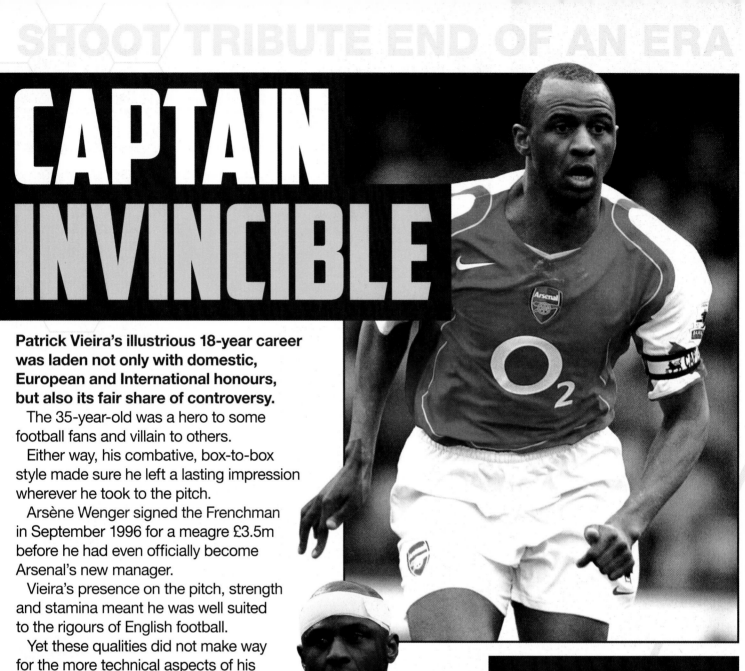

Patrick Vieira's illustrious 18-year career was laden not only with domestic, European and International honours, but also its fair share of controversy.

The 35-year-old was a hero to some football fans and villain to others.

Either way, his combative, box-to-box style made sure he left a lasting impression wherever he took to the pitch.

Arsène Wenger signed the Frenchman in September 1996 for a meagre £3.5m before he had even officially become Arsenal's new manager.

Vieira's presence on the pitch, strength and stamina meant he was well suited to the rigours of English football.

Yet these qualities did not make way for the more technical aspects of his game such as composure, touch, balance, an eye for goal (he was more than capable of the odd screamer) and a wonderful ability to elegantly stride past defenders with the ball. Indeed, he was the complete dictatorial midfield general.

Early on in his Arsenal days, Vieira lacked self-control, and on no fewer than eight occasions in the league he found himself taking an early bath after overstepping the mark.

Reckless tackles and the flailing

WHAT HIS BOSSES SAY...

"His career is sensational. He was an exceptional player for us"
Arséne Wenger, *his boss at Arsenal*

"Patrick is a world-class midfielder with a winner's mentality."
Roberto Mancini, *his boss at Man City*

FACT FILE

Position: Midfielder
Birth Date: June 23, 1976
Birth Place:
Dakar, Senegal
Clubs: Cannes, AC Milan, Arsenal, Juventus, Inter Milan, Manchester City
International:
France (107 caps, 6 goals)
Honours:
Arsenal: Premier League (3); FA Cup (4); Community Shield (4).
Inter Milan: Serie A (4); Italian Super Cup (2); Italian Cup (1); Champions League (1).
Man City: FA Cup (1).

retaliatory arms were becoming a destructive part of Vieira's game and it all came to a head in the second game of the 2000-01 season.

It was his second sending off in three days and there was much talk of him quitting English football, so fed up was he of red cards and what he perceived to be victimisation from Premier League officials.

Vieira has now taken up a community role in a capacity created specifically to keep him at Manchester City.

It speaks volumes for Vieira, the man and the footballer, that the richest club in the world not only wanted him in the first place, but also wanted to go to such lengths to keep him around.

DID YOU KNOW?

During his nine years at Arsenal, Vieira made 406 appearances – ten of them as a substitute – and scored 33 goals. Gunners fans voted him their fifth-best player of all-time in a 2008 poll.

MAGNIFICENT SEVEN
HIGHLIGHTS FROM VIEIRA'S CAREER

KEANE CRUNCH Bumping foreheads, snarling in one another's faces and brawling in the Highbury tunnel before a game in 2005 – these are some moments Vieira will be remembered for when people talk about his battles with Man United captain Roy Keane. Anyone who gives Keane a run for his money has to be some player!

SPURS GOAL Not exactly noted for his scoring ability, the Frenchman hit some gems. One standout was for Arsenal against Tottenham at White Hart Lane when the Gunners clinched the league in 2004.

THE INVINCIBLES Vieira was given the captain's armband for the 2002-03 campaign. The following year he led Arsenal to an historic unbeaten season, culminating in yet another Premier League winner's medal. He was skipper of the side during their unprecedented 49-match unbeaten run – a feat which had never been seen before or since. As captain of that team, dubbed The Invincibles, Vieira secured his place as an Arsenal legend.

PARTING SHOT A fitting finale to his career for the North London club was on a sodden surface at Cardiff's Millennium Stadium in the 2005 FA Cup Final against Man United. His last-ever kick for Arsenal in a shoot-out won the game.

FRENCH STAR On the international stage, Vieira racked up more than a century of international caps for his country, picking up the 1998 World Cup and European Championship in 2000. He notched six goals in that time and was made captain following Zinedine Zidane's retirement.

ITALIAN JOB After going to Italy in 2005, Vieira was yet again among the silverware, winning four consecutive league titles with Inter Milan and helping them on their way to the Champions League trophy 2010.

CITY SLICKER Vieira returned to the Premier League with Manchester City in January 2010, a signing that proved immensely popular among the fans. Although often on the bench, Vieira was a favourite at Eastlands and always given a rousing reception during his 39-game spell at the club.

MUSIC MEN

TOP FOOTBALLERS WHO HAVE PROVED THEY ARE IN TUNE...

Many footballers fancy themselves as singers – but Kevin Rutkiewicz has left them all in his wake.

Not content with appearing in the Scottish Premier League, the defender hasn't just written and recorded his own album, but he's also toured with Ultravox and Live Aid legend Midge Ure.

The Dunfermline captain, who has also turned out for Aberdeen and St. Johnstone, released his first album, Handwritten, to critical acclaim. Spending his childhood listening to popular 60s, 70s and present day music played by parents Ernest and Matilda, Kevin picked up the guitar during an injury spell at Aberdeen. At St. Johnstone he was invited to play a charity concert and since then has played the King Tuts Wah Wah Hut venue in his native Glasgow. Born in Scotland with Polish ancestry - his Grandfather moved to the UK during World War II - Kevin has been likened to other Scottish acts such as Paolo Nutini and the Proclaimers.

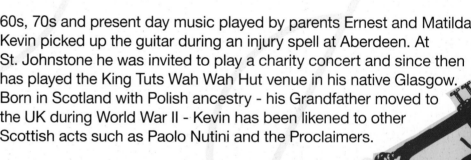

BLOWING HOT!

Former Newcastle United winger Nobby Solano is a hot-shot with the trumpet and even formed his own Salsa band!

The Peru midfielder, who also had spells with Aston Villa, West Ham and Hull City, used to take his trumpet into the dressing room at St. James' Park and has even given Salsa lessons!

Solano also used to pull a prank on his former boss Sir Bobby Robson: "I used to phone up his mobile and play my trumpet down the phone to him.

"He didn't know it was me, but one day somebody told him that I knew how to play the trumpet. So then he worked out that it must be me. He called me up and just laughed with me down the phone."

TUNING IN...

Former Norwich City forward **Paul McVeigh** spent his time off the pitch learning to play both the guitar and piano! The Northern Ireland player, who also turned out for Burnley, Luton and Spurs, reckons he strummed the strings and tinkled the ivories because he liked learning new things!

Man United and England striker **Wayne Rooney** is known to have a pretty wide choice of favourite music – some not so great – but he's also reportedly keen on learning how to drum!

Team play could mean a whole lot more to **Didier Drogba** and **Florent Malouda** after reports that they wanted to set up a rock group at Chelsea. With Drogba on bass and Malouda on the drums they also hoped to rope in captain John Terry to sing!

England forward **Joe Cole** started to learn guitar during his time at Chelsea. The midfielder took lessons from Patrick Mascall, multi-talented strummer with group Van Tramp.

Defender **Titus Bramble** and midfielder **Lee Cattermole** became big mates with Take That star Robbie Williams after meeting up with him in America. Evidently the Robster's football was a lot better than their singing…

ROCK ON ROSICKY!

Arsene Wenger would throw a wobbler if he watched Tomas Rosicky perform off the pitch - on guitar for a punk rock group! The midfielder picked up the electric axe during the Czech Republic's Footballer of the Year ceremony to play with Lou Fananek Hagen and his band Tri Sestry. The crowd reckon he wasn't that bad and there are reports that he has been practising his plucking since his public debut on stage.

MIDFIELD MARVEL

damien rice 0

U2
THE BEST OF 1980-1990

Midfielder Andy Reid has pulled strings in a few midfields – and he's also a bit handy when it comes to pulling them on a guitar.

The Republic of Ireland star has been known to cover artists as diverse as Damien Rice through to U2 and The Dubliners and has even performed before big crowds on stage in public.

Reid, who has turned out for the likes of Nottingham Forest, Tottenham, Sunderland and Blackpool, admitted: "I have written some songs but not many people get to hear them. I don't think many will! I think some are OK, some are pretty poor. I am certainly not recording any while I play football. Afterwards, who knows what will happen?"

WE WERE THERE...

2003: All round Thierry Henry's for a quick game of football on the computer? Well, let's be honest here, *Shoot* was holed up in a flash London hotel for the interview with the Arsenal and France legend – a very pleasant afternoon with an amiable guy. *Shoot's* man on the spot got a bit carried away as the pair battled it out on screen and had it been a real match the referee might have decided there was a little too much va va voom and swiftly dealt a red card to the scribe! Yes things were that serious, but it's not often you get to challenge one of the true stars of world football to FIFA Football!

CLASSIC IMAGE

100 TOP PLAYERS

100 TOP PLAYERS

PAGE 52 - 67
SHOOT'S TOP 100 PLAYERS

Many of the world's best players turn out in the Premier League. Shoot's put together this list of 100 stars who have made a name in England. They are in no particular order, we don't claim they are the 100 best in the competition today, and they may not even be in England's top-flight at this current moment.

But they are players who have made - or are making - an important contribution to their team and the game of football. Not all of them have turned out for their countries but we have indicated their nationalities should they pull on an international shirt.

PAGE 68 - 69
SHOOT'S TOP INTERNATIONAL PLAYERS

Ask anyone on the planet to name the No.1 player in the world and they are likely to say Lionel Messi. But the Barcelona forward isn't the only international star whose boots are loaded with talent.

Shoot's put together a list of a few other players you might just want to consider if you put together a World Best XI...

DIRK KUYT

Position: Striker
Birth date: July 22, 1980
Birth place: Katwijk, Holland
Height: 1.83m (6ft)
Clubs: Quick Boys, Utrecht, Feyenoord, Liverpool
International: Holland

Did you Know?
Liverpool paid around £10m to buy Kuyt in summer 2006. He had previously been linked with a move to Newcastle United.

NEMANJA VIDIC

Position: Defender
Birth date: Oct 21, 1981
Birth place: Titovo Uzice, Yugoslavia
Height: 1.89m (6ft 2in)
Clubs: Red Star Belgrade, Spartak Subotica (loan), Spartak Moscow, Manchester United
International: Serbia

Did you Know?
Vidic was appointed Man United captain at the start of season 2010-11.

FLORENT MALOUDA

Position: Midfielder
Birth date: June 13, 1980
Birth place: Cayenne, France
Height: 1.77m (5ft 9in)
Clubs: Chateauroux, Guingamp, Lyon, Chelsea
International: France

Did you Know?
Malouda scored France's only goal at the 2010 World Cup finals in South Africa when his country exited at the group stage.

DIMITAR BERBATOV

Position: Striker
Birth date: Jan 30, 1981
Birth place: Blagoevgrad, Bulgaria
Height: 1.89m (6ft 2in)
Clubs: Pirin Blagoevgrad, CSKA Sofia, Bayer Leverkusen, Tottenham, Manchester United
International: Bulgaria

Did you Know?
Spurs bought him for £10.9m in 2006 and sold him to United for £30.75m.

JOHN TERRY

Position: Defender
Birth date: Dec 7, 1980
Birth place: Barking, Essex
Height: 1.87m (6ft 1in)
Clubs: Chelsea, Nottingham Forest (loan)
International: England

Did you Know?
JT was first appointed England captain by Steve McClaren in 2006. He scored on his debut wearing the armband, in a friendly against Greece.

WAYNE ROONEY

Position: Striker
Birth date: Oct 24, 1985
Birth place: Croxteth, Liverpool
Height: 1.76m (5ft 9in)
Clubs: Everton, Man United
International: England

Did you Know?
United paid £26.5m to buy Rooney from Everton when he was still just 18-years-old. It was then the highest fee paid for a player under the age of 20.

BREDE HANGELAND

Position: Defender
Birth date: June 20,1981
Birth place: Houston, USA
Height: 1.94m (6ft 4in)
Clubs: Viking, FC Copenhagen, Fulham
International: Norway

Did you Know?
Boss Roy Hodgson, who was Hangeland's manager at Viking, signed him for Fulham in January 2008. He cost £2.5m and is now rated three times that.

VINCENT KOMPANY

Position: Defender
Birth date: April 10, 1986
Birth place: Uccle, Belgium
Height: 1.9m (6ft 3in)
Clubs: Anderlecht, Hamburg, Manchester City
International: Belgium

Did you Know?
Kompany, who can play in defence or midfield, joined City in summer 2008 for £6m. He was their fans' and players' Player of the Year for season 2010-11.

PETR CECH

Position: Keeper
Birth date: May 20, 1982
Birth place: Plzen, Czechoslovakia
Height: 1.96m (6ft 5in)
Clubs: Chmel Blsany, Sparta Prague, Rennes, Chelsea
International: Czech Republic

Did you Know?
He kept 25 Premier League clean sheets as Chelsea won the 2004-05 title.

NANI

Position: Winger
Birth date: Nov 17, 1986
Birth place: Praia, Cape Verde
Height: 1.75m (5ft 9in)
Clubs: Sporting Lisbon, Manchester United
International: Portugal

Did you Know?
Nani was voted United's Players' Player of the Year for 2010-11. He was also in the PFA's Premier League team of the year.

KEVIN NOLAN

Position: Midfielder
Birth date: June 24, 1982
Birth place: Liverpool
Height: 1.83m (6ft)
Clubs: Bolton, Newcastle United, West Ham
International: England

Did you Know?
Newcastle sold Nolan, their captain, to West Ham for £4m in summer 2011 - the same fee they had paid to buy the former Bolton trainee in January 2009.

JOE HART

Position: Keeper
Birth date: April 19, 1987
Birth place: Shrewsbury, Shropshire
Height: 1.96m (6ft 5in)
Clubs: Shrewsbury, Tranmere (loan), Blackpool (loan), Birmingham City (loan), Manchester City
International: England

Did you Know?
Hart was Birmingham City's Player of the Year during his loan in 2009-10.

ASHLEY COLE

Position: Defender
Birth date: Dec 20, 1980
Birth place:
Stepney, East London
Height: 1.76m (5ft 9in)
Clubs: Arsenal, Crystal Palace (loan), Chelsea
International: England

Did you Know?
In 2010, Cole became the first player to win six FA Cup medals. He has won three with both Arsenal and Chelsea.

YAYA TOURE

Position: Midfielder
Birth date: May 13, 1983
Birth place: Sekoura Bouake, Ivory Coast
Height: 1.92m (6ft 3in)
Clubs: Beveren, Metalurh, Olympiacos, Monaco, Barcelona, Manchester City
International: Ivory Coast

Did you Know?
Toure cost Man City £24m when he signed from Barca in 2010, a year after brother Kolo joined the club.

JACK RODWELL

Position: Midfielder
Birth date: March 11, 1991
Birth place:
Southport, Lancashire
Height: 1.88m (6ft 2in)
Clubs: Everton
International: England

Did you Know?
Rodwell, who can also play as a central defender, has turned out for England at Under-16, 17, 19 and 21 levels. He made his Everton debut at the age of 16.

PEPE REINA

Position: Keeper
Birth date: Aug 31, 1982
Birth place: Madrid
Height: 1.88m (6ft 2in)
Clubs: Barcelona, Villarreal, Liverpool
International: Spain

Did you Know?
Reina, who signed for Liverpool in 2005, was part of Spain's winning squads at World Cup 2010 and Euro 2008. He played just one game, in the Euros.

SAMIR NASRI

Position: Midfielder
Birth date: June 26, 1987
Birth place: Marseille, France
Height: 1.77m (5ft 10in)
Clubs: Marseille, Arsenal, Man City
International: France

Did you Know?
Although he failed to make France's World Cup 2010 squad, he was recalled by new boss Laurent Blanc for Euro 201 qualifiers and has since captained the side.

ASHLEY YOUNG

Position: Winger
Birth date: July 9, 1985
Birth place:
Stevenage, Hertfordshire
Height: 1.75m (5ft 9in)
Clubs: Watford, Aston Villa, Manchester United
International: England

Did you Know?
Young cost Villa almost £10m from Watford in 2007 and was sold to Manchester United for around £15m in summer 2011.

CHARLIE ADAM

Position: Midfielder
Birth date: Dec 10, 1985
Birth place:
Dundee, Scotland
Height: 1.85m (6ft 1in)
Clubs: Rangers, Ross County (loan), St. Mirren (loan), Blackpool (loan), Blackpool, Liverpool
International: Scotland

Did you Know?
Blackpool bought Adam for £500,000 and sold him to Liverpool for £7m.

SYLVAIN DISTIN

Position: Defender
Birth date: Dec 16, 1977
Birth place:
Bagnolet, France
Height: 1.93m (6ft 4in)
Clubs: Gueugnon, Paris Saint Germain, Newcastle (loan), Manchester City, Portsmouth, Everton.
International: France

Did you Know?
Distin won the FA Cup with Portsmouth and the French Cup with Gueugnon.

DARREN BENT

Position: Striker
Birth date: Feb 6, 1984
Birth place:
Tooting, South London
Height: 1.8m (5ft 11in)
Clubs: Ipswich, Charlton,
Tottenham, Sunderland
Aston Villa
International: England

Did you Know?
Bent was a shock £24m
buy for Villa in January
2011. He scored nine goals
in his first 16 games.

ROBIN VAN PERSIE

Position: Striker
Birth date: Aug 6, 1983
Birth place:
Rotterdam, Holland
Height: 1.83m (6ft)
Clubs: Feyenoord,
Arsenal
International: Holland

Did you Know?
The 18 Premier League
goals van Persie scored in
2010-11 was a new personal
best, as were the 22 he
scored in all competitions.

GARETH BALE

Position: Winger
Birth date: July 16, 1989
Birth place: Cardiff, Wales
Height: 1.83m (6ft)
Clubs: Southampton,
Tottenham
International: Wales

Did you Know?
Bale was voted Professional
Footballers' Association
Players' Player of the Year
in 2011. He was the fourth
Spurs player to win the
prestigious award.

RAFAEL VAN DER VAART

Position: Midfielder
Birth date: Feb 11, 1983
Birth place:
Heemskerk, Holland
Height: 1.77m (5ft 9in)
Clubs: Ajax, Hamburg,
Real Madrid, Tottenham
International: Holland

Did you Know?
Van der Vaart has two
Dutch League titles from his
time at Ajax. He cost Spurs
£8m as the summer 2010
transfer window closed.

ANDREY ARSHAVIN

Position: Striker/Winger
Birth date: May 29, 1981
Birth place:
St. Petersburg, Russia
Height: 1.72m (5ft 7in)
Clubs: Zenit St. Petersburg,
Arsenal
International: Russia

Did you Know?
During his time with St.
Petersburg Arshavin won
the Russian League, Premier
League Cup, Super Cup,
UEFA Cup and Super Cup.

JONAS GUTIERREZ

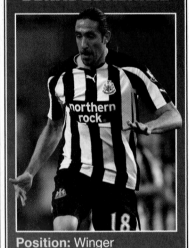

Position: Winger
Birth date: July 5, 1983
Birth place:
Saenz Pena, Argentina
Height: 1.83m (6ft)
Clubs: Velez Sarsfield,
Mallorca, Newcastle United
International: Argentina

Did you Know?
Although noted as a tricky
winger playing on the left
at club level, Jonas is often
played at right back by
Argentina.

FRANK LAMPARD

Position: Midfielder
Birth date: June 20, 1978
Birth place:
Romford, Essex
Height: 1.84m (6ft)
Clubs: West Ham, Swansea
City (loan), Chelsea
International: England

Did you Know?
The Premier League's
Player of the Decade from
2000-09, Lampard is the
highest scoring midfielder
in Chelsea's history.

GAEL CLICHY

Position: Defender
Birth date: July 25, 1985
Birth place:
Toulouse, France
Height: 1.76m (5ft 9in)
Clubs: Cannes, Arsenal,
Manchester City
International: France

Did you Know?
During his time at Arsenal,
Clichy won the Premier
League and Community
Shield in 2004 and the
FA Cup in 2005.

MICHAEL ESSIEN

Position: Midfielder
Birth date: Dec 3, 1982
Birth place: Accra, Ghana
Height: 1.78m (5ft 10in)
Clubs: Bastia, Lyon, Chelsea
International: Ghana

Did you Know?
Essien won two league titles in France before winning the Premier League with Chelsea in 2006 and 2010. He has won three FA Cups and a League Cup.

RAUL MEIRELES

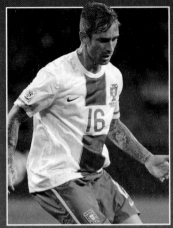

Position: Midfielder
Birth date: March 17, 1983
Birth place: Porto, Portugal
Height: 1.8m (5ft 11in)
Clubs: Boavista, Aves (loan), Porto, Liverpool, Chelsea
International: Portugal

Did you Know?
During his time with Porto Meireles won four League titles in a row from 2006-09. He also lifted the Portuguese Cup and Super Cup, both three times.

CHARLES N'ZOGBIA

Position: Winger
Birth date: May 28, 1986
Birth place: Harfleur, France
Height: 1.71m (5ft 8in)
Clubs: Le Havre, Newcastle United, Wigan, Aston Villa
International: France

Did you Know?
N'Zogbia was bought from Newcastle by Wigan for £6m in 2009 and sold to Aston Villa in summer 2011 for £9.5m.

ALEX SONG

Position: Defender
Birth date: Sept 9, 1987
Birth place: Douala, Cameroon
Height: 1.84m (6ft)
Clubs: Bastia, Arsenal, Charlton (loan)
International: Cameroon

Did you Know?
His cousin is former Liverpool and West Ham defender Rigobert Song. They have played in the same Cameroon side.

LIAM RIDGEWELL

Position: Defender
Birth date: July 21, 1984
Birth place: Bexleyheath, Kent
Height: 1.88m (6ft 2in)
Clubs: Aston Villa, Bournemouth (loan), Birmingham City
International: England

Did you Know?
In 2007 he became the first player in 23 years to move from Aston Villa to rivals Birmingham City.

STEWART DOWNING

Position: Winger
Birth date: July 22, 1984
Birth place: Middlesbrough
Height: 1.8m (5ft 11in)
Clubs: Middlesbrough, Sunderland (loan), Aston Villa, Liverpool
International: England

Did you Know?
Just two years after joining Aston Villa for around £12m, Downing transferred to Liverpool for a fee of around £20m.

SEBASTIAN LARSSON

Position: Midfielder
Birth date: June 6, 1985
Birth place: Eskilstuna, Sweden
Height: 1.78m (5ft 10in)
Clubs: Arsenal, Birmingham, Sunderland
International: Sweden

Did you Know?
Larsson spent a season on loan with Birmingham City before making the move permanent for a fee of around £1m in 2007.

BRANISLAV IVANOVIC

Position: Defender
Birth date: Feb 22, 1984
Birth place: Sremska Mitrovia, Yugoslavia
Height: 1.88m (6ft 2in)
Clubs: Remont, Srem, OFK Beograd, Lokomotiv Moscow, Chelsea
International: Serbia

Did you Know?
When he joined Chelsea for £9m in 2008, Ivanovic's transfer fee was believed to be a Russian record.

JORDAN HENDERSON

Position: Midfielder
Birth date: June 17, 1990
Birth place: Sunderland
Height: 1.82m (6ft)
Clubs: Sunderland, Coventry (loan), Liverpool
International: England

Did you Know?
Sunderland's Young Player of the Year in 2010 and 2011, Henderson moved to Liverpool for £16m in summer 2011. Made his England debut in 2010.

BEN FOSTER

Position: Keeper
Birth date: April 3, 1983
Birth place: Leamington Spa, Warwickshire
Height: 1.93m (6ft 4in)
Clubs: Stoke, Bristol City (loan), Wrexham (loan), Man United, Watford (loan), Birmingham City, West Brom (loan)
International: England

Did you Know?
Foster was also loaned to three non-league clubs.

STEVEN TAYLOR

Position: Defender
Birth date: Jan 23, 1986
Birth place: Greenwich, London
Height: 1.88m (6ft 2in)
Clubs: Newcastle United, Wycombe (loan)
International: England

Did you Know?
Taylor was born in London because his father was working there. He grew up on Tyneside and has always supported Newcastle.

MAXI RODRIGUEZ

Position: Winger
Birth date: Jan 2, 1981
Birth place: Rosario, Argentina
Height: 1.8m (5ft 11in)
Clubs: Newell's Old Boys, Espanyol, Atletico Madrid, Liverpool
International: Argentina

Did you Know?
When Fernando Torres left Atletico Madrid for Liverpool Rodrigues took over as the club's captain.

GARY CAHILL

Position: Defender
Birth date: Dec 19, 1985
Birth place: Sheffield
Height: 1.88m (6ft 2in)
Club: Aston Villa, Burnley (loan), Sheffield United (loan), Bolton
International: England

Did you Know?
Although he went to Sheffield United on loan Cahill had been brought up as a Wednesday fan in his home city.

AARON HUGHES

Position: Defender
Birth date: Nov 8, 1979
Birth place: Cookstown, Northern Ireland
Height: 1.83m (6ft)
Club: Newcastle United, Aston Villa, Fulham
International: Northern Ireland

Did you Know?
Hughes made his debut for Newcastle United against Barcelona when he was just 18-years-old.

NICOLAS ANELKA

Position: Striker
Birth date: March 14, 1979
Birth place: Versailles, France
Height: 1.85m (6ft 1in)
Clubs: Paris Saint Germain, Arsenal, Real Madrid, Liverpool (loan) Man City, Fenerbahce, Bolton, Chelsea
International: France

Did you Know?
He won the Premier League with Arsenal and Chelsea.

JAMES COLLINS

Position: Defender
Birth date: Aug 23, 1983
Birth place: Newport, Wales
Height: 1.93m (6ft 4in)
Club: Cardiff City, West Ham, Aston Villa
International: Wales

Did you Know?
Since 2001 Collins has played from Under-19s through to the senior side for Wales and has also captained the full team.

CHRIS SAMBA

Position: Defender
Birth date: March 28, 1984
Birth place: Creteil, France
Height: 1.93m (6ft 4in)
Clubs: Sedan, Hertha Berlin, Blackburn Rovers
International: DR Congo

Did you Know?
Samba underwent a five-day trial with Blackburn before joining them for a bargain £400,000 in January 2007, when Mark Hughes was manager.

ROGER JOHNSON

Position: Defender
Birth date: April 28, 1983
Birth place: Ashford, Surrey
Height: 1.91m (6ft 3in)
Clubs: Wycombe, Cardiff City, Birmingham City, Wolves
International: England

Did you Know?
Following Birmingham's relegation from the Premier League in 2011, Johnson was sold to Wolves for £7m.

DJ CAMPBELL

Position: Striker
Birth date: Nov 12, 1981
Birth place: Hammersmith, West London
Height: 1.78m (5ft 10in)
Clubs: Brentford, Birmingham City, Leicester City, Blackpool (loan), Derby (loan), Blackpool, QPR
International: England

Did you Know?
He was 23-years-old when Brentford gave him his break in League Football.

BACARY SAGNA

Position: Defender
Birth date: Feb 14, 1983
Birth place: Bourgogne, France
Height: 1.76m (5ft 9in)
Clubs: Auxerre, Arsenal
International: France

Did you Know?
Sagna was Auxerre's Player of the Year when he left for Arsenal in 2007. He was named in the Premier League teams of the year for 2007-08 and 2010-11.

MARTIN SKRTEL

Position: Defender
Birth date: Dec 15, 1984
Birth place: Handlova, Czechoslovakia
Height: 1.91m (6ft 3in)
Clubs: Trencin, Zenit Saint Petersburg, Liverpool
International: Slovakia

Did you Know?
Rafael Benitez signed Skrtel for Liverpool for £6.5m in January 2008. The defender played in all of the club's 2010-11 league games.

KEVIN DAVIES

Position: Striker
Birth date: March 26, 1977
Birth place: Sheffield
Height: 1.83m (6ft)
Clubs: Chesterfield, Southampton, Blackburn Rovers, Southampton, Millwall (loan), Bolton
International: England

Did you Know?
Davies won his first cap for his country in October 2010 at the age of 33, in a Euro 2012 qualifying game.

GARETH BARRY

Position: Midfielder
Birth date: Feb 23, 1981
Birth place: Hastings, East Sussex
Height: 1.83m (6ft)
Clubs: Aston Villa, Manchester City
International: England

Did you Know?
Barry has captained his country as stand-in skipper on a number of occasions during the reign of manager Fabio Capello.

MATT JARVIS

Position: Winger
Birth date: May 22, 1986
Birth place: Middlesbrough
Height: 1.7m (5ft 7in)
Clubs: Gillingham, Wolves
International: England

Did you Know?
Wolves fans and players both handed their Player of the Year awards to Jarvis at the end of 2010-11, the season in which he also made his full debut for England.

CESC FABREGAS

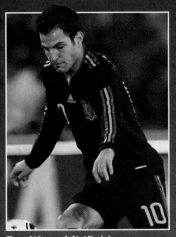

Position: Midfielder
Birth date: May 4, 1987
Birth place:
Vilassar de Mar, Spain
Height: 1.75m (5ft 9in)
Club: Arsenal, Barcelona
International: Spain

Did you Know?
Fabregas began his career as a trainee in Barcelona's youth academy but signed for Arsenal at the age of 16 – and made his debut a month after arriving.

DAVID SILVA

Position: Midfielder
Birth date: Jan 8, 1986
Birth place:
Arguineguin, Spain
Height: 1.7m (5ft 7in)
Clubs: Valencia, Eibar
(loan), Celta Vigo (loan),
Manchester City
International: Spain

Did you Know?
Silva, a £24m signing by Man City in 2010, won Euro 2008 and World Cup 2010 with Spain.

DARREN FLETCHER

Position: Midfielder
Birth date: Feb 1, 1984
Birth place:
Dalkeith, Scotland
Height: 1.84m (6ft)
Club: Manchester United
International: Scotland

Did you Know?
The Scotland captain won his fourth Premier League title with United at the end of 2010-11. He has also won an FA Cup, two League Cups and a European Cup.

TIM HOWARD

Position: Keeper
Birth date: March 6, 1979
Birth place:
New Jersey, USA
Height: 1.91m (6ft 3in)
Club: North Jersey
Imperials, MetroStars,
Manchester United, Everton
International: USA

Did you Know?
For three seasons, from 2008-09 to 10-11, Howard has played in every Premier League game for Everton.

HEURELHO GOMES

Position: Keeper
Birth date: Feb 15, 1981
Birth place:
Joao Pinheiro, Brazil
Height: 1.19m (6ft 3 in)
Clubs: Cruzeiro, PSV
Eindhovthen, Tottenham
International: Brazil

Did you Know?
The keeper built a great reputation at PSV where he helped the Dutch side to four titles. He has also won the Brazilian league.

PHIL NEVILLE

Position: Midfielder
Birth date: Jan 21, 1977
Birth place:
Bury, Manchester
Height: 1.8m (5ft 11in)
Clubs: Man United, Everton
International: England

Did you Know?
Gary Neville's younger brother won 59 England caps between 1996 and 2007. He has said he will never turn down the chance to represent his country.

FABRICIO COLOCCINI

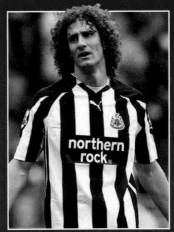

Position: Defender
Birth date: Jan 22, 1982
Birth place:
Cordoba, Argentina
Height: 1.83m (6ft)
Clubs: Boca Juniors, AC
Milan, San Lorenzo (loan),
Alaves (loan), Atletico
Madrid (loan), Deportivo,
Newcastle United
International: Argentina

Did you Know?
Coloccini was appointed Newcastle captain in 2011.

DAVID VAUGHAN

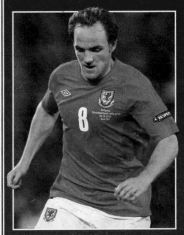

Position: Midfielder
Birth date: Feb 18, 1983
Birth place:
Abergele, Wales
Height: 1.7m (5ft 7in)
Clubs: Crewe, Real
Sociedad, Blackpool,
Sunderland
International: Wales

Did you Know?
Vaughan was signed for Real Sociedad by former Wales defender Chris Coleman, who was sacked.

SCOTT PARKER

Position: Midfielder
Birth date: Oct 13, 1980
Birth place:
Lambeth, South London
Height: 1.75m (5ft 9in)
Clubs: Charlton, Norwich (loan) Chelsea, Newcastle United, West Ham, Tottenham
International: England

Did you Know?
The 2011 Football Writers' Footballer of the Year has won England caps playing for four different clubs.

FERNANDO TORRES

Position: Striker
Birth date: March 20, 1984
Birth place:
Fuenlabrada, Spain
Height: 1.83m (6ft)
Clubs: Atletico Madrid, Liverpool, Chelsea
International: Spain

Did you Know?
Torres set a new British transfer record when he moved from Liverpool to Chelsea for £50m in the January window 2011.

YOUSSOUF MULUMBU

Position: Midfielder
Birth date: Jan 25, 1987
Birth place: Kinshasa, Zaire
Height: 1.77m (5ft 10in)
Clubs: Paris Saint Germain, Amiens (loan),West Brom
International: DR Congo

Did you Know?
Mulumbu cost the Baggies just £175,000 after a short loan. His value is now far in excess of that fee and he was given a four-year contract at the Hawthorns.

ANDY CARROLL

Position: Striker
Birth date: Jan 6, 1989
Birth place: Gateshead
Height: 1.91m (6ft 3in)
Clubs: Newcastle, Preston (loan), Liverpool
International: England

Did you Know?
Carroll was Britain's most expensive transfer for just a few hours when he joined Liverpool for £35m. The fee was topped by Fernando Torres's £50m move.

JOSE ENRIQUE

Position: Defender
Birth date: Jan 25, 1986
Birth place:
Valencia, Spain
Height: 1.84m (6ft)
Clubs: Levante, Valencia, Celta Vigo (loan), Villarreal, Newcastle United, Liverpool
International: Spain

Did you Know?
The full back cost Newcastle £6m in 2007 when Sam Allardyce was still Magpies manager.

BRAD FRIEDEL

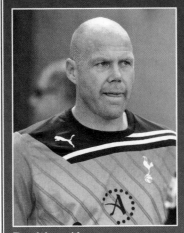

Position: Keeper
Birth date: May 18, 1971
Birth place:
Lakewood, USA
Height: 1.88m (6ft 2in)
Clubs: Brondby (loan), Galatasaray, Columbus Crew, Liverpool, Blackburn, Aston Villa, Tottenham
Infernational: England

Did you Know?
Friedel set a record of being Villa's oldest-ever player at 40 years and four days.

CLINT DEMPSEY

Position: Striker-midfielder
Birth date: March 9, 1983
Birth place:
Nacogdoches, Texas
Height: 1.85m (6ft 1in)
Club: New England Revolution, Fulham
International: USA

Did you Know?
Dempsey's 12 goals in 2010-11 made him Fulham's highest overall scorer in the Premier League with a total of 33 in five years.

MORTEN GAMST PEDERSEN

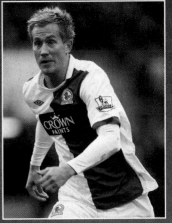

Position: Midfielder
Birth date: Sept 8, 1981
Birth place:
Vadso, Norway
Height: 1.83m (6ft)
Club: Tromso, Blackburn
International: Norway

Did you Know?
Pedersen joined Rovers in 2004 and until the end of 2010-11 season had made 227 Premier League appearances for the side, scoring 31 goals.

JACK WILSHERE

Position: Midfielder
Birth date: Jan 1, 1992
Birth place:
Stevenage, Hertfordshire
Height: 1.73m (5ft 8in)
Clubs: Arsenal,
Bolton (loan)
International: England

Did you Know?
When Wilshere made his full England debut against Hungary in August, 2010, he was the tenth youngest Three Lions player.

PHIL BARDSLEY

Position: Defender
Birth date: June 28, 1985
Birth place:
Salford, Manchester
Height: 1.8m (5ft 11in)
Clubs: Man United, Royal Antwerp (loan), Burnley (loan), Rangers (loan), Aston Villa (loan), Sheffield United (loan), Sunderland
International: Scotland

Did you Know?
He qualifies for Scotland as his father is from Glasgow.

ROBERT HUTH

Position: Defender
Birth date: Aug 18, 1984
Birth place:
Berlin, Germany
Height: 1.91m (6ft 3in)
Clubs: Chelsea, Middlesbrough, Stoke City
International: Germany

Did you Know?
Huth was Stoke City's Players' and Fans' Player of the Year for 2011 and also made Potteries Footballer of the Year.

KENWYNE JONES

Position: Striker
Birth date: Oct 5, 1984
Birth place: Port Fortin, Trinidad and Tobago
Height: 1.88m (6ft 2 in)
Club: Southampton, Sheffield Wednesday (loan) Stoke City (loan), Sunderland, Stoke City
International:
Trinidad and Tobago

Did you Know?
Jones cost Stoke £8m from Sunderland, a club record.

RYAN SHAWCROSS

Position: Defender
Birth date: Oct 4, 1987
Birth place: Chester
Height: 1.91m (6ft 3in)
Clubs: Manchester United, Royal Antwerp, Stoke City
International: England

Did you Know?
Sir Alex Ferguson, who sold the player for £2m in 2008, has first option to buy back Shawcross for Manchester United if the defender ever leaves Stoke City.

SEAMUS COLEMAN

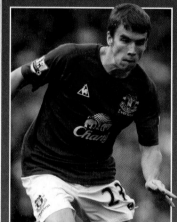

Position: Defender
Birth date: Oct 11, 1988
Birth place:
Donegal, Ireland
Height: 1.77m (5ft 9in)
Club: Sligo, Everton, Blackpool (loan)
International:
Republic of Ireland

Did you Know?
Coleman was bought from Sligo Rovers for £150,00 in 2009. He helped Blackpool to the Premier League.

JAVIER HERNANDEZ

Position: Striker
Birth date: June 1, 1988
Birth place:
Guadalajara, Mexico
Height: 1.75m (5ft 9in)
Clubs: Guadalajara, Manchester United
International: Mexico

Did you Know?
Hernandez, nicknamed Chicharito, hit 20 goals in 2010-11, his first season with Man United, 13 of them in the Premier League.

PAUL ROBINSON

Position: Defender
Birth date: Dec 14, 1978
Birth place:
Watford, Hertfordshire
Height: 1.75m (5ft 9in)
Clubs: Watford, West Brom, Bolton
International: England

Did you Know?
Bolton signed Robinson on a season-long loan and then paid £1m to make his move from West Brom permanent in 2010.

ROB GREEN

Position: Keeper
Birth date: Jan 18, 1980
Birth place:
Chertsey, Surrey
Height: 1.91m (6ft 3in)
Clubs: Norwich, West Ham
International: England

Did you Know?
Norwich sold Green to West Ham for £2m in summer 2006. He had made his full England debut the previous year, having played at youth level for his country.

BENOIT ASSOU-EKOTTO

Position: Defender
Birth date: March 24, 1984
Birth place: Arras, France
Height: 1.78m (5ft 10in)
Clubs: Lens, Tottenham
International: Cameroon

Did you Know?
Assou-Ekotto played the full 90 minutes of Cameroon's three first round games at the 2010 World Cup finals in South Africa. He missed that year's Africa Cup of Nations due to injury.

GLEN JOHNSON

Position: Defender
Birth date: Aug 23, 1984
Birth place:
Greenwich, South London
Height: 1.82m (5ft 11in)
Clubs: West Ham United, Millwall (loan), Chelsea, Portsmouth, Liverpool
International: England

Did you Know?
When Johnson moved from West Ham to Chelsea for £6m in 2003 he was Roman Abramovich's first big buy.

MARC ALBRIGHTON

Position: Midfielder
Birth date: Nov 18, 1989
Birth place:
Tamworth, Staffordshire
Height: 1.75m (5ft 9in)
Club: Aston Villa
International: England

Did you Know?
Albrighton was a Villa supporter as a boy and joined the club at the age of eight. In 2010, he made his Under-21 debut and first Premier League start.

NIGEL DE JONG

Position: Midfielder
Birth date: Nov 30, 1984
Birth place:
Amsterdam, Holland
Height: 1.74m (5ft 8in)
Clubs: Ajax, Hamburg, Manchester City
International: Holland

Did you Know?
City forked out around £18m to buy De Jong in January 2009. He played in the Holland side that lost the 2010 World Cup Final.

ALI AL-HABSI

Position: Keeper
Birth date: Dec 30, 1981
Birth place: Muscat, Oman
Height: 1.94m (6ft 4in)
Clubs: Al-Midhaibi, Al-Nasr, Lyn, Bolton, Wigan
International: Oman

Did you Know?
Al-Habsi spent 2010-11 on loan at Wigan before they bought him from Bolton. During that time he won the club's Player of the Season award.

DANNY MURPHY

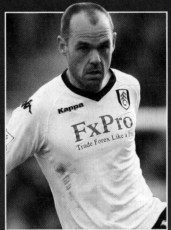

Position: Midfielder
Birth date: March 18, 1977
Birth place: Chester
Height: 1.75m (5ft 9in)
Clubs: Crewe, Liverpool, Charlton Athletic, Tottenham, Fulham
International: England

Did you Know?
During his time at Liverpool he won six trophies: FA Cup, League Cup (twice), Community Shield, UEFA Cup and UEFA Super Cup.

ZAT KNIGHT

Position: Defender
Birth date: May 2, 1980
Birth place:
Solihull, West Midlands
Height: 1.98m (6ft 6in)
Clubs: Fulham, Peterborough (loan), Aston Villa, Bolton
International: England

Did you Know?
Knight has made more than 250 Premier League appearances for Fulham, Aston Villa and Bolton.

LUKA MODRIC

Position: Midfielder
Birth date: Sept 9, 1985
Birth place:
Zadar, Yugoslavia
Height: 1.73m (5ft 8in)
Clubs: Dinamo Zagreb,
Zrinjski Mostar (loan), Inter
Zapresic (loan), Tottenham
International: Croatia

Did you Know?
He won three titles in a row
with Dinamo Zagreb before
becoming a Spurs club
record £16.5m buy in 2008.

RYAN NELSEN

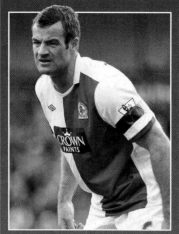

Position: Defender
Birth date: Oct 18, 1977
Birth place:
Christchurch, New Zealand
Height: 1.83m (6ft)
Clubs: Christchurch United,
DC United, Blackburn
International: New Zealand

Did you Know?
Nelsen arrived at Blackburn
on a free transfer from
America's DC United in
2005 and has captained
both club and country.

JUSSI JAASKELAINEN

Position: Keeper
Birth date: April 19, 1975
Birth place:
Mikkeli, Finland
Height: 1.91m (6ft 3in)
Clubs: Mikkelin Palloilijat,
Vaasan Palloseura, Bolton
International: Finland

Did you Know?
Jaaskelainen has played
more than 500 games for
Bolton since joining them in
1997. He quit international
football after 56 caps.

LEE CHUNG-YONG

Position: Winger
Birth date: July 2, 1988
Birth place:
Seoul, South Korea
Height: 1.8m (5ft 11in)
Clubs: FC Seoul, Bolton
International: South Korea

Did you Know?
At the end of his first
season at Bolton, following
a £2.2m transfer, he was
named Bolton Player of the
Year, Players' Player of the
Year and best newcomer.

MAROUANE CHAMAKH

Position: Striker
Birth date: Jan 10, 1984
Birth place:
Tonneins, France
Height: 1.88m (6ft 2in)
Clubs: Bordeaux, Arsenal
International: Morocco

Did you Know?
Arsenal trailed Chamakh for
more than a year, failed in
a £5m bid for him in 2009,
but then landed him on
a free in 2010 when his
Bordeaux contract ran out.

JOEY BARTON

Position: Midfielder
Birth date: Sept 2, 1982
Birth place:
Huyton, Liverpool
Height: 1.8m (5ft 11in)
Clubs: Manchester City,
Newcastle United, QPR
International: England

Did you Know?
Barton stayed at Newcastle
when they were relegated in
2009 but missed a lot of the
Championship-winning
season through injury.

PATRICE EVRA

Position: Defender
Birth date: May 15, 1981
Birth place: Dakar, Senegal
Height: 1.73m (5ft 8in)
Clubs: Marsala, Monza,
Nice, Monaco, Man United
International: France

Did you Know?
Evra arrived at Man United
in 2006 and has so far
picked up four Premier
League titles, three League
Cups, a European Cup and
FIFA Club World Cup.

ASAMOAH GYAN

Position: Striker
Birth date: Nov 22, 1985
Birth place: Accra, Ghana
Height: 1.8m (5ft 11in)
Clubs: Liberty
Professionals, Udinese,
Modena (loan), Rennes,
Sunderland
International: Ghana

Did you Know?
After starring at World Cup
2010 in South Africa, Gyan
became Sunderland's
record buy for £13m.

ADEL TAARABT

Position: Midfielder
Birth date: May 24, 1989
Birth place: Taza, Morocco
Height: 1.8m (5ft 11in)
Clubs: Lens, Tottenham, Queens Park Rangers
International: Morocco

Did you Know?
The 2010-11 Football League Player of the Year had loan spells with both Spurs and QPR before signing permanent deals with the clubs.

CHEIK TIOTE

Position: Midfielder
Birth date: June 21, 1986
Birth place: Yamoussoukro, Ivory Coast
Height: 1.75m (5ft 9in)
Clubs: Anderlecht, Roda (loan), Twente, Newcastle
International: Ivory Coast

Did you Know?
Tiote won the Dutch league with Twente – under former England boss Steve McClaren – before joining Newcastle for £4m in 2010.

SHANE LONG

Position: Striker
Birth date: Jan 22, 1987
Birth place: Gortnahoe, Ireland
Height: 1.79m (5ft 11in)
Clubs: Cork City, Reading, West Brom
International: Republic of Ireland

Did you Know?
After two sub appearances for Cork, Long was part of the deal that took striker Kevin Doyle to Reading.

THEO WALCOTT

Position: Striker
Birth date: March 16, 1989
Birth place: Stanmore, West London
Height: 1.75m (5ft 9in)
Clubs: Southampton, Arsenal
International: England

Did you Know?
Walcott, who cost Arsenal £12m in 2006, has played at Under-16, 17, 19 and 21 levels right through to the full England senior side.

DIDIER DROGBA

Position: Striker
Birth date: March 11, 1978
Birth place: Abidjan, Ivory Coast
Height: 1.89m (6ft 2in)
Clubs: Le Mans, Guingamp, Marseille, Chelsea
International: Ivory Coast

Did you Know?
Drogba has won African and Ivorian Footballer of the Year awards twice, and won the Premier League Golden Boot in 2007 and 2010.

CARLOS TEVEZ

Position: Striker
Birth date: Feb 5, 1984
Birth place: Buenos Aires, Argentina
Height: 1.73m (5ft 8in)
Clubs: Boca Juniors, Corinthians, West Ham, Man United, Man City
International: Argentina

Did you Know?
In the Premier League, Tevez has worn the same number on his shirt – 32 – at all three of his clubs.

PETER ODEMWINGIE

Position: Striker
Birth date: July 15, 1981
Birth place: Tashkent, Russia
Height: 1.82m (5ft 11in)
Clubs: Bendel Insurance, La Louviere, Lille, Lokomotiv Moscow, West Brom
International: Nigeria

Did you Know?
He scored 15 Premier League goals in his first season with West Brom.

LEIGHTON BAINES

Position: Defender
Birth date: Dec 11, 1984
Birth place: Kirkby, Merseyside
Height: 1.7m (5ft 7in)
Clubs: Wigan, Everton
International: England

Did you Know?
Baines helped Wigan rise from the third tier of English football to the Premier League and then played 72 games for them in the top-flight.

DAVID VILLA

Position: Striker
Birth date: Dec 3, 1981
Birth place:
Langreo, Spain
Height: 1.75m (5ft 9in)
Clubs: Sporting Gijon,
Zaragoza, Valencia,
Barcelona
International: Spain

Did you Know?
Villa is Spain's record
goal scorer, his first 75
internationals producing
an amazing 47 goals.

DAVID DE GEA

Position: Keeper
Birth date: Nov 7, 1990
Birth place: Madrid, Spain
Height: 1.93m (6ft 4in)
Clubs: Atletico Madrid,
Manchester United
International: Spain

Did you Know?
His £18m move from
Atletico to United in
summer 2011 made him the
second most expensive
keeper in the world, behind
£33m Gianluigi Buffon.

FRANCK RIBERY

Position: Winger
Birth date: April 7, 1983
Birth place:
Boulogne-sur-Mer, France
Height: 1.7m (5ft 7in)
Clubs: Boulogne, Ales,
Brestois, Metz, Galatasaray,
Marseille, Bayern Munich
International: France

Did you Know?
Ribery has twice been
France Footballer of the
Year and won the German
award in 2008.

MAICON

Position: Defender
Birth date: July 26, 1981
Birth place:
Novo Hamburgo, Brazil
Height: 1.84m (6ft)
Clubs: Cruzeiro, Monaco,
Inter Milan
International: Brazil

Did you Know?
Maicon has a Brazil title to
his name, four Serie A wins,
two Italian Cups, a
European Cup and Club
World Cup victory.

VICTOR VALDES

Position: Keeper
Birth date: Jan 14, 1982
Birth place:
Barcelona, Spain
Height: 1.83m (6ft)
Club: Barcelona
International: Spain

Did you Know?
Five La Liga titles, three
Champions Leagues wins,
four Spanish Super Cups
and a World Cup medal are
among the shot-stoppers
awards so far!

BASTIAN SCHWEINSTEIGER

Position: Midfielder
Birth date: Aug 1, 1984
Birth place:
Kolbermoor, Germany
Height: 1.83m (6ft)
Club: Bayern Munich
International: Germany

Did you Know?
In more than 350 games for
Bayern, Schweinsteiger has
won five Bundesligas, five
German Cups and two
League Cups and played
in two World Cup finals.

ALEXANDRE PATO

Position: Striker
Birth date: Sept 2, 1989
Birth place: Parana, Brazil
Height: 1.79m (5ft 10in)
Clubs: Internacional,
AC Milan
International: Brazil

Did you Know?
Pato's goal for Internacional
in the 2006 FIFA Club World
Cup helped him beat Pelé's
record as the youngest
scorer in FIFA competitions.
He was 17 years, 102 days.

PEDRO

Position: Midfielder
Birth date: July 28, 1987
Birth place:
Tenerife, Canaries
Height: 1.7m (5ft 7in)
Club: Barcelona
International: Spain

Did you Know?
Pedro's first three seasons
in the Barca first-team
produced three La Liga
titles, two Champions
Leagues, a Copa del Rey
and two Spain Super Cups.

ANGEL DI MARIA

Position: Winger
Birth date: Feb 14, 1988
Birth place:
Rosario, Argentina
Height: 1.8m (5ft 11in)
Clubs: Rosario Central, Benfica, Real Madrid
International: Argentina

Did you Know?
Di Maria, whose praises have been sung by Diego Maradona, joined Madrid in summer 2010 in a deal worth an initial £20.3m.

NEYMAR

Position: Striker
Birth date: Feb 5, 1992
Birth place:
Sao Paulo, Brazil
Height: 1.74m (5ft 9in)
Club: Santos
International: Brazil

Did you Know?
Some of Europe's biggest clubs joined a queue to sign the teenager with Chelsea, Man United, Juventus, Real Madrid and both Milan clubs watching him.

GONZALO HIGUAIN

Position: Striker
Birth date: Dec 10, 1987
Birth place: Brest, France
Height: 1.84m (6ft)
Clubs: River Plate, Real Madrid
International: Argentina

Did you Know?
Born in France, Higuain holds a French passport but doesn't speak the language. He returned to his parents' homeland of Argentina as a baby.

EDEN HAZARD

Position: Midfielder
Birth date: Jan 7, 1991
Birth place:
La Louviere, Belgium
Height: 1.72m (5ft 8in)
Club: Lille
International: Belgium

Did you Know?
Highly rated Hazard was 2011 Ligue One Player of the Year having won the French league's Young Player award in both 2009 and 2010.

ALEXIS SANCHEZ

Position: Striker
Birth date: Dec 19, 1988
Birth place:
Tocopilla, Chile
Height: 1.69m (5ft 7in)
Clubs: Cobreloa, Udinese, Colo-Colo (loan), River Plate (loan), Barcelona
International: Chile

Did you Know?
Sanchez joined Barca in summer 2011 for a fee that could reach £30m-plus depending on his progress.

THOMAS MULLER

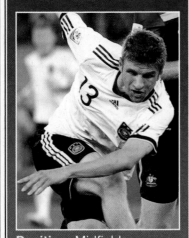

Position: Midfielder
Birth date: Sept 13, 1989
Birth place:
Weilheim, Germany
Height: 1.86m (6ft 1in)
Club: Bayern Munich
International: Germany

Did you Know?
Muller was Best Young Player at World Cup 2010 and won the Golden Boot after scoring five goals. He had made his Germany debut just months earlier.

CRISTIANO RONALDO

Position: Winger
Birth date: Feb 5, 1985
Birth place: Madeira
Height: 1.86m (6ft 1in)
Clubs: Sporting Lisbon, Man United, Real Madrid
International: Portugal

Did you Know?
Ronaldo set a new world record transfer when he moved from Man United to Real Madrid for £80m in 2009. United had bought him for £12m in 2003.

KAKA

Position: Midfielder
Birth date: April 22, 1982
Birth place: Brasilia, Brazil
Height: 1.85m (6ft 1in)
Clubs: Sao Paulo, AC Milan, Real Madrid
International: Brazil

Did you Know?
Manchester City failed in an amazing £100m bid to buy Kaka from AC Milan in January 2009. He joined Real Madrid six months later for £56m.

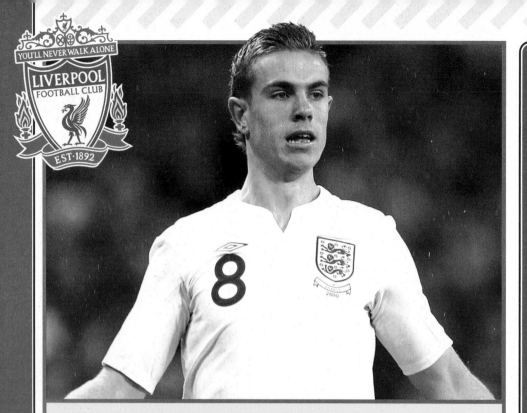

WHAT HE SAID "They have paid a lot of money for me but that shows Liverpool have faith. I always work hard, you have just got to get on with things and make sure you are confident."

HIS BOSS SAYS...

"Jordan is very mature for his age. He is respectful and his principles and everything else on and off the pitch are exemplary. Not only is he a talented footballer, he's a really good person as well. He loves his football and he is very appreciative of what Sunderland have done for him."

Kenny Dalglish,
Liverpool manager

DID YOU KNOW?

Henderson, who was under contract at Sunderland to 2015, was the club's Young Player of the Year for 2010.

Kenny Dalglish's rebuilding project will include some major redevelopments at Liverpool– but Jordan Henderson could prove to be the foundation stone.

Henderson will cost up to £20m from Sunderland and many expect him to be groomed as the eventual replacement for the amazing Steven Gerrard.

That's a very tough act to follow but one which the 21-year-old is willing to try and live up to.

Having played alongside Gerrard on his full England debut during last year's friendly against France, Henderson admits: "He's one of the best players in the world. Hopefully I can learn a lot from him."

Henderson admits that it wont be easy to follow in Stevie G's boots but he is planning to try his best. His first task is to cement a regular place in the Anfield first-team.

"Am I confident I can do that? If I work hard I will get my chance and take it," he said. "All I care about is making sure I am in the starting eleven and playing regularly."

FACT FILE

JORDAN BRIAN HENDERSON
Position: Midfielder
Height: 1.82m (6ft)
Birth Date: June 17, 1990
Birth Place: Sunderland
Clubs: Sunderland, Coventry (loan), Liverpool
International: England

NEW PREMIER LEAGUE STARS
BLACK CAT TURNS RED

Newcastle fans have mixed feelings when it comes to signing French players – but will hope Yohan Cabaye is one of their better buys.

While the Geordies fondly remember the flowing locks and mercurial skills of David Ginola, they also wince at the arrival of miss-firing Gallic striker Stephane Guivarc'h who hit a goal on his debut, played three more games and was sold.

Cabaye, 25, has been capped four times by France and is destined to take up the role occupied by former captain Kevin Nolan, although the new man is more of a box-to-box player.

Cabaye, who cost £4.5m, said: "It's my first transfer and I am joining a big, legendary club. There was talk of Liverpool and Arsenal but Newcastle were the club who made the move for me and I really like Alan Pardew's strategy and how he told me he wants to play.

"I have enjoyed great times with Lille but the time is right now to test myself against the best and playing for Newcastle United in the Premier League does just that."

Cabaye was convinced by former Newcastle winger Charles N'Zogbia to move to St. James' Park.

FACT FILE
YOHAN CABAYE
Position: Midfielder
Height: 1.75m (5ft 9in)
Birth Date: Jan 14, 1986
Birth Place: Tourcoing, France
Clubs: Lille, Newcastle
International: France

WHAT HE SAID "I am going to play in the best championship in the world for a club who want to get back into Europe within a year and one who are building an ambitious team."

HIS BOSS SAYS...
"We are delighted to have signed Yohan on a five-year contract. He has a first class pedigree having proved himself at the top level in France, both for his club and the national team. He will add great quality to our squad and I am really looking forward to working with him."
Alan Pardew,
Newcastle manager

DID YOU KNOW?
Cabaye was born in the same month of the same year as Newcastle's England defender Steven Taylor. And both players have captained their country's Under-21 sides.

NEW PREMIER LEAGUE STARS
CABAYE DRIVER

WHAT HE SAID "I know there's competition for places. It's up for grabs in every position and it's only healthy for the squad. I've got to keep training hard, working my way up."

HIS BOSS SAYS...

"The area we had to work hardest with Phil was to convince him he would get enough football. The other thing I explained to him was that we are always trying to look ahead towards the team of the future rather than the team of the present."

Sir Alex Ferguson,
Manchester United manager

DID YOU KNOW?

Jones had only recently signed a new five-year deal with Blackburn. United's offer was simply too good to refuse and Rovers said they would not stand in the way of his development.

The arrival of Phil Jones at Manchester United could see the Old Trafford club developing the careers of England's central defence for the next few years.

But it won't be Rio Ferdinand you can expect to see line up alongside Jones in a Three Lions shirt.

Jones and Chris Smalling are the two new boys on the block at United, two big hopes for England and two potential successors for Ferdinand and his current partner Nemanja Vidic.

Jones, 19, cost a staggering £16.5m from Blackburn after just 35 Premier League games for Rovers. But the England Under-21 star admits: "I aspire to follow John Terry, Michael Dawson and Rio Ferdinand. I always watch what they do and learn from them."

And Smalling, still only 21, a £10m arrival from Fulham in 2010, added: "It's brilliant Phil and I will be playing at the same club. I've really enjoyed playing with him for England and hopefully we can get better for club and country."

Jones admits: "It's amazing where I have come from and where I am now."

FACT FILE

PHILIP ANTHONY JONES
Position: Defender
Height: 1.8m (5ft 11in)
Birth Date: Feb 21, 1992
Birth Place:
Preston, Lancashire
Clubs: Blackburn Rovers, Manchester United
International: England

NEW PREMIER LEAGUE STARS
UNITED KEEP UP WITH THE JONES

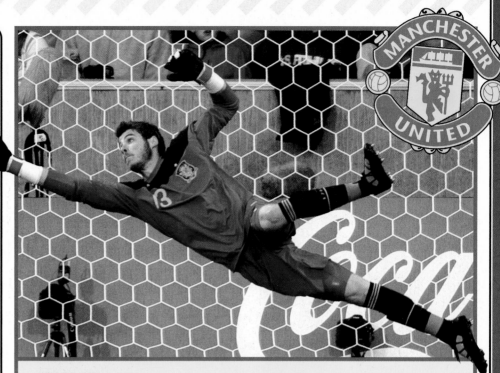

Less than two years ago David De Gea was a relatively unknown reserve for Atletico Madrid.

Now he is a full international with Spain and set to play in the world's most competitive league with one of the planet's biggest clubs.

De Gea's £18m move to Manchester United is a big gamble on a player who has played just 57 games in La Liga and it is one that Sir Alex Ferguson will hope comes off.

Keeper hasn't always been United's strongest point but in recent years Edwin van der Sar has set standard previously only reached by Peter Schmeichel.

De Gea is a novice in goalkeeping terms so has plenty of time to improve. But he will be expected to make an immediate impact at the Theatre of Dreams.

Having played for his country at every level from Under-17 to Under-21 he knows about pressure and was a key member of the Spain side that won the 2011 European Under-21 Championships.

De Gea admits: "I liked watching Schmeichel when I was young and also Van der Sar, both are among the best I have seen. I need to keep on working hard, as I am still in the outset of my career, and I still have much to do."

FACT FILE

DAVID DE GEA
Position: Goalkeeper
Height: 1.93m (6ft 4in)
Birth Date: Nov 7, 1990
Birth Place: Madrid, Spain
Clubs: Atletico Madrid, Manchester United
International: Spain

WHAT HE SAID "Manchester United are one of the best clubs in the world and it's an important step in my career. I'm going to do as well as possible there and try to succeed."

HIS BOSS SAYS...

"We worked on the deal for quite a while. He's young, quick, and has very good composure. He's an outstanding replacement for Edwin van der Sar. Obviously we have signed David De Gea as the main choice, but it is an open door for me."
Sir Alex Ferguson,
Manchester United manager

DID YOU KNOW?

In 2009, Wigan agreed a loan deal with a view to a permanent transfer for De Gea. But the move fell through at the last minute when Atletico decided the player was too important to allow to leave.

NEW PREMIER LEAGUE STARS
STEPPING UP A GEA

MY FAVOURITE PLAYER

TOP PLAYERS NAME THE PREMIER LEAGUE STARS THEY ADMIRE

RYAN GIGGS

"When he plays it is like he is 20 because he's everywhere. You have to be careful with him."

Emmanuel Eboue, *Arsenal and Ivory Coast defender*

DIDIER DROGBA

"He is a great finisher and creates a lot of chances for himself with his movement. You will not find another player like him again, he is a one-off. His way of playing, turning, finishing in the box – he is unique."

Mido, *former Tottenham and Egypt striker*

WAYNE ROONEY

"I don't think I ever look forward to facing him. He is the best striker in the world, a great player."

Tim Howard, *Everton and USA keeper*

JAVIER HERNANDEZ

"Chicharito's become a hugely important player for United where he has scored so many important goals. He is very fast, a very intelligent striker and adapted well at a great club in a short space of time."

Lionel Messi, *Barcelona*

MICHAEL DAWSON

"He's a great player. He is great for us and amazing in front of me. He pushes us a bit and we need players like him."

Heurelho Gomes, *Spurs and Brazil keeper*

BEN FOSTER

"He is tremendous. He should be England's No.1. He does it week in, week out, day in, day out. In matches and in training."

Craig Gardner, *Sunderland midfielder*

TOP TRIVIA

WHO'S THAT?

Darts ace James Wade thought he was about to be plagued by a troublesome fan when he was out shopping.

"I was in the local chemist and this guy went to me, 'All right, Wadey?' I thought it was someone trying to be a pest. So I replied, 'All right'," said Wade, a double Grand Prix winter. Wade's other half at the time, TV presenter Helen Chamberlain, then got a text from the "pest" asking how rude was her boyfriend. He'd only cold-shouldered one of his neighbours in the Surrey town – England and Chelsea defender John Terry, a massive darts fan!

COMPARE THE PLAYER DOT COM!

England winger Adam Johnson is known by his team-mates as Meerkat – as they reckon he's the spitting image of Alexander Orlov, the meerkat from the TV adverts!

GOOD SPORT

There was no escaping sport in Gareth Bale's family.

The Wales and Tottenham defender's dad, Frank, played amateur football.

Gareth's mum, Debbie, loved netball and hockey and his Uncle Chris turned out for a number of clubs, including home town side Cardiff City.

CAT NAP

Keeper Richard Kingson is nicknamed The Cat – but it's nothing to do with his performances in goal whilst at Blackpool.

His team-mates reckon the Ghana international is just like a four-legged feline and can sleep anywhere.

They reckon he even fell to sleep playing a Poker event!

CARPING ON ABOUT FISH

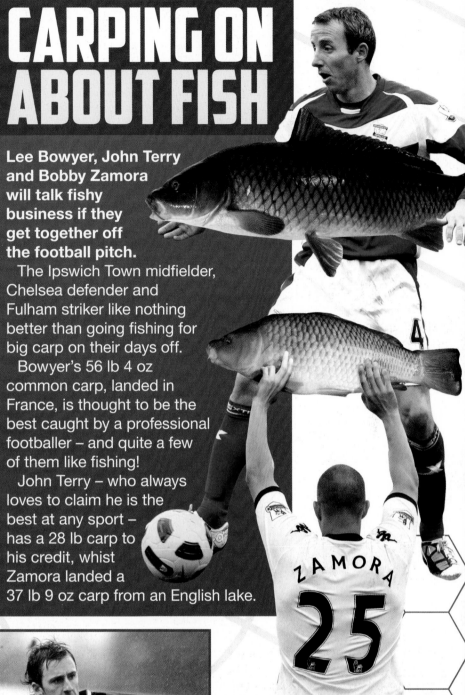

Lee Bowyer, John Terry and Bobby Zamora will talk fishy business if they get together off the football pitch.

The Ipswich Town midfielder, Chelsea defender and Fulham striker like nothing better than going fishing for big carp on their days off.

Bowyer's 56 lb 4 oz common carp, landed in France, is thought to be the best caught by a professional footballer – and quite a few of them like fishing!

John Terry – who always loves to claim he is the best at any sport – has a 28 lb carp to his credit, whist Zamora landed a 37 lb 9 oz carp from an English lake.

STUDS UP!

Striker Jack Midson borrowed a pair of boots from a team-mate and scored a hat-trick!

After being out on loan, he returned to Oxford United to make his first appearance for almost four months and took the boots from centre half Harry Worley as his studs were not long enough for the wet pitch.

It was his first treble as a professional and his final goal earned a 4-3 victory at Torquay.

REC🛡️RD BREAKERS

THE EARLY YEARS

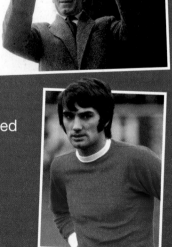

1907-08 United finished nine points clear of Aston Villa and Manchester City to clinch their first-ever title. Ernest Mangnall was United's manager.

1910-11 Just one point separated Champions United and runners-up Villa with Sunderland third, seven points behind the winners. Mangnall was again the boss at Old Trafford.

1951-52 Sir Matt Busby's first title as boss with United four points clear of both Spurs and Arsenal.

1955-56 Busby's second top-flight title saw them 11 points ahead of both Blackpool and Wolves.

1956-57 Busby's third as United retained a title for the first time. Spurs and Preston were eight points adrift.

1964-65 United's closest victory so far, beating Leeds on goal difference. Third-placed Chelsea were five points off the pace.

1966-67 George Best lifted his second United title as they finished four points clear of both Nottingham Forest and Tottenham. Busby's final championship win.

THE EARLY PREMIER LEAGUE YEARS

1992-93

The first-ever Premiership, Sir Alex Ferguson's first-ever English title and the start of Man United's glory, glory years. United were ten points clear of Aston Villa and 12 in front of Norwich. Eric Cantona was the star player in only his first season with united.

1993-94

Man United notched a staggering 92 points to see off Blackburn Rovers who amassed 84, the total which had won the crown for Fergie the previous season. Bryan Robson was captain.

1995-96

The arrival of Fergie's Fledglings as his crop of academy youngsters scored a Double and lifted the league, four points ahead of Newcastle and 11 in front of Liverpool. Cantona had returned from his kung-fu kick ban.

1996-97

Super sub Ole Gunnar Solskjaer, the baby faced assassin, top scored for the Red Devils with 18 as they again beat Newcastle, this time by seven points. Arsenal were third on goal difference.

1998-99

They won the league just one point ahead of Arsenal and with four more than Chelsea. They were also inspired to the FA Cup and European Cup by the skills of Teddy Sheringham.

TURN THE PAGE TO SEE HOW MAN UNITED WON THE ENGLISH LEAGUE SEVEN MORE TIMES

THE NEW MILLENNIUM

1999-00

A staggering 18 points separated Man United and Arsenal at the end of the season with Leeds a further four points adrift. Dwight Yorke was their smiling assassin with 20 goals.

2000-01

Three titles in a row meant a new English record for Sir Alex Ferguson. Ten points ahead of Arsenal and 11 in front of Liverpool. Gary Neville was their most used player with 32 appearances.

2002-03

Arsenal were again the bridesmaids, five points behind United with Newcastle a further nine behind the Gunners. Holland striker Ruud van Nistelrooy was the golden boy with 25 league goals, a staggering 44 in total.

2006-07

It was the 31-goal partnership of Cristiano Ronaldo and Wayne Rooney that helped United to the top, six points ahead of Chelsea. A further five points adrift were Liverpool.

2007-08

A league and Champions League Double, the title being clinched on the final day with a 2-0 victory at Wigan. Giggs scored and Ronaldo struck from the penalty spot, his 31st League goal of the season as he lifted the Golden Boot.

2008-09

Eleven titles for Fergie and an 18th by United to equal the English best held by Liverpool. It was Ryan Giggs' 11th title, also a record.

THE RECORD - 2010-11

United began the season by beating Chelsea in the Community Shield at Wembley – and ended it by pushing the Blues into second spot in the league. The crunch game came in the third-last match of the season when United beat Chelsea 2-1 at Old Trafford to virtually seal the title. One point at Blackburn in the penultimate game of the campaign sealed the trophy. Berbatov's 20 Premier League goals were significant as Fergie's men finished nine points ahead of both Chelsea and Man City.

EUROPE'S FINEST

Manchester United set a new English record when they collected their 19th league title in 2010-11. But they are still a long way behind some of the other top sides in Europe. Here are the best, and their nearest challengers…

ITALY

JUVENTUS 27

AC MILAN 18

INTER MILAN 18

HOLLAND

AJAX 29

PSV EINDHOVEN 21

SCOTLAND

RANGERS 54

CELTIC 42

AUSTRIA

RAPID VIENNA 32

AUSTRIA VIENNA 23

BELGIUM

ANDERLECHT 30

CLUB BRUGGE 13

ENGLAND

MAN UNITED 19

LIVERPOOL 18

PORTUGAL

BENFICA 32

PORTO 28

NORWAY

ROSENBORG 22

FREDRIKSTAD 9

SWITZERLAND

GRASSHOPPERS 27

SERVETTE 17

SPAIN

REAL MADRID 31

BARCELONA 21

GREECE

OLYMPIAKOS 38

PANATHINAIKOS 20

SHOOT'S ULTIMATE BOOK OF FOOTBALL 2012

TURKEY

FENERBAHCE 18

GALATASARAY 17

GERMANY

BAYERN MUNICH 22

NUREMBERG 9

RUSSIA

SPARTAK MOSCOW 19

LOKOMOTIV MOSCOW 19

CSKA MOSCOW 19

DYNAMO MOSCOW 19

POLAND

GORNIK ZABRZE 14

RUCH CHORZOW 14

WISLA KRAKOW 13

FRANCE

ST. ETIENNE 10

MARSEILLE 10

NANTES 8

ALBANIA

KF TIRANA 24

DINAMO 18

ISRAEL

MACCABI TEL AVIV 18

HAPOEL TEL AVIV 13

CZECH REPUBLIC

SPARTA PRAGUE 11

SLAVIA PRAGUE 3

DENMARK

FC COPENHAGEN 30

BRONDBY 10

FACT

Four Moscow sides dominate the haul of Russian league titles. The country's Premier League was formed in 2001 and Spartak have won nine titles.

FACT

Albania feature in our list because Tirana are one of the most successful clubs in Europe thanks to their 24-title haul.

FACT

Denmark's FC Copenhagen was formed in 1992 when KB and Boldklubben amalgamated. The 30 titles is a combined total of their victories.

FACT

Rangers' 54 titles is a world record. They won their first in 1891 and latest of three in a row in 2011.

FACT

Sir Alex Ferguson has been in charge for 12 of Manchester United's record 19 title wins. All of his victories have been in the Premier League.

FACT

Ryan Giggs has scored a club best of 69 goals during their 12 Premier League titles, one more than Ole Gunnar Solskjaer.

KING SALOMON
AND KALOU WANTS TO KEEP ON RULING!

Salomon Kalou failed to lift any silverware last season – and that is something he's not used to!

He's one of Chelsea's unsung heroes yet he has a Premier League title, two FA Cups and a League Cup to his name since arriving at Stamford Bridge in 2006.

"I know we have won trophies but the hunger is still there," said the Ivory Coast forward. "We have good professionals, good experience and people who are hungry to win."

Kalou's often in the shade of some big-money, big-name megastars, but his statistics show he's been an important part of the Blues' squad. He's made more than 200 appearances and clocked up around a goal every four games since he was bought from Dutch side Feyenoord for £9m by former boss Jose Mourinho.

Kalou's path to a regular first-team place hasn't been easy with six more managers passing through the Stamford Bridge gates during his time in West London. "Every time you get a new coach you have to prove yourself all over again. It was easier with Carlo [Ancelotti] as I knew how he wanted me to play," said Kalou who has also played for Mourinho, Avram Grant, Luiz Felipe Scolari, Guus Hiddink and Andre Villas-Boas.

Kalou added: "When you play for Chelsea it's not always about fun. You have to do whatever it takes to win. When you win the Premier League you have to retain it to prove it wasn't luck."

Having played and scored in the 2008 African Cup of Nations and the 2010 World Cup finals, the Ivorian has appeared on the biggest football stages in the world.

The headlines are usually about his club and country team-mate Drogba and other Blues stars but that won't stop Kalou battling for his own glory.

Now Kalou reckons: "I want to be one of Chelsea's most important players and fulfil the expectations that people have of me. I'm going to have to work hard to score goals and set more up."

Kalou could get carried away with the lifestyle of a top footballer but his feet are firmly nailed to the ground.

"I always dreamed of being a footballer," he admits. "I get to be part of something millions of people aspire to be part of. I travel the world, play in packed stadiums and the money is good too! I really do appreciate my life, especially when I think back to all the hard times growing up to get here. That keeps me humble."

FACT FILE
SALOMON ARMAND MAGIOIRE KALOU
Position: Winger
Height: 1.86m (6ft 1in)
Birth Date: August 5, 1985
Birth Place: Oume, Ivory Coast
Clubs: Mimosa, Excelsior (loan), Feyenoord, Chelsea
International: Ivory Coast

DID YOU KNOW?
The Ivorian stripped off to be photographed naked for a campaign to raise awareness about male cancer. "The photoshoot was real fun, it will certainly make some ladies look at me differently," he smiled.

TOP TRIVIA!

LAUGH, CRY OR JUST BE TOTALLY AMAZED AT THE CRAZY WORLD OF FOOTBALL...

NOT THE TICKET

Mario Balotelli has a habit of picking up cards on the pitch – and tickets off it!

The Italian striker has been quite popular with Premier League referees' notebooks and even more popular with parking wardens!

Balotelli's arrival at Manchester City saw him pick up a wad of parking tickets and he's had to retrieve his flash Maserati from the impound yard a number of times.

CUP POTTY

Stoke City's appearance in the FA Cup Final resulted in a wedding being cancelled... by the bride!

Footie-mad Suzanne Dono, 29, had followed the Potters all her life and wasn't going to miss the big day out at Wembley against Manchester City. She told hubby-to-be Steve Wakefield she had known him just three years compared to her love of Stoke which had been almost 30!

WAYNE'S WORLD

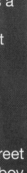

England and Man United striker Wayne Rooney can't get enough football – but away from the pitch he's hooked on TV soaps and kids' films!

The Roonster is a massive fan of Coronation Street and EastEnders and just loves to chill out with wife Coleen to watch the programmes.

His favourite Street character is bad boy David Platt, although he also rates Steve McDonald and Becky. Although Rooney insists he is a northern boy, who doesn't even like travelling to London, his top EastEnder is Max Branning.

The England star is also hooked on The Lion King, his son Kai's favourite movie.

THE GREATEST!

A poll of football supporters voted Liverpool's comeback against AC Milan in the 2005 Champions League Final as the greatest moment in the event's history.

The Reds were 3-0 down at half-time, came back to 3-3 and then won the penalty shoot-out.

Second in the poll was Man United's victory in 1999 when they were 1-0 down and won 2-1 with two goals in time added-on. No surprise that Sir Alex Ferguson got the nod as the greatest manager.

VIOLENT VIDS

Football computer games make people more aggressive than violent games, according to boffins. Psychologists at Huddersfield University reckon that closer-to-life soccer games gets us going more than the likes of Call of Duty and Grand Theft Auto!

CHIPPING IN

Graham Alexander has notched more than 1,000 games – and reckons it's got nothing to do with special diets.

The defender, who has appeared for Burnley, Scunthorpe, Luton and Preston, reckons he's played on to 40 because of his mother's chips!

"I think it's all the burger and chips I ate from my mum and dad when I was a kid that has helped me," said the Coventry born player. The former Scotland star admits he was 23 before he knocked back the footballer's favourite of pasta! Alexander made his Scunthorpe debut in 1988 when he was just 17. He is only the second English outfield player to reach 1,000 games.

TUNED IN...

Guitar-playing Shane Long has hit the right notes with his goal-scoring exploits.

The Republic of Ireland striker has been immortalised in a song called 'The Ballad of Shane Long'. Bought by Reading from Cork in 2005, Long has been given his tribute by Willie Dunne and the Corrigan brothers and the song's got a cult following on the Internet.

Both Dunne and Long hail from Gortnahoe in Tipperary. Dunne said: "It's an honour to record a song about an outstanding player like Shane."

OUT OF TUNE...

David Luiz was an instant smash hit with Chelsea fans following his arrival in West London.

But the Brazilian didn't show off the Samba beat when he went through his club initiation ceremony. All Chelsea arrivals have to perform a dance or song in front of their new team-mates and Luiz's was evidently so bad that his new friends couldn't end the performance quick enough.

WE WERE THERE...

2002: Finding the two Nevilles, Phil and Gary, with a chair in the middle of a field is not something that you see everyday! The brothers were still team-mates when *Shoot* turned up for this photo-interview in Cheshire, fixed up with their then boot-sponsor Diadora. As usual, they were both good value for quotes and had forthright views on football happenings of the day. Surprisingly the same can't be said for their fellow Manchester United star Roy Keane – the Republic of Ireland midfielder failed to turn up!

CLASSIC IMAGE

19 YEARS OF THE PREMIER LEAGUE

YOUR GUIDE TO ALL THE SEASONS SO FAR

Everyone knows Sir Alex Ferguson and his Manchester United side are the kings of England's top-flight.

But do you remember the other sides who have won the Premier League? Can you name the top scorers and major transfers from the 19 seasons played so far? Do you remember where you favourite side finished every season, or how many points they scored?

All of the important answers to the biggest questions are contained in the next twenty pages...

BARCLAYS PREMIER LEAGUE

IT'S A FACT

Just one manager was sacked during the season: Chelsea's Ian Porterfield.

Forest's legendary boss, Brian Clough, retired at the end of the campaign.

FINAL TABLE

	P	GD	PTS
Man United	42	36	84
Aston Villa	42	17	74
Norwich City	42	-4	72
Blackburn	42	22	71
QPR	42	8	63
Liverpool	42	7	59
Sheff Wed	42	4	59
Tottenham	42	-6	59
Man City	42	5	57
Arsenal	42	2	56
Chelsea	42	-3	56
Wimbledon	42	1	54
Everton	42	-2	53
Sheff United	42	1	52
Coventry	42	-5	52
Ipswich	42	-5	52
Leeds	42	-5	51
Southampton	42	-7	50
Oldham	42	-11	49
Crystal Palace	42	-13	49
Middlesbrough	42	-21	44
Nottingham Forest	42	-21	40

ELSEWHERE...

FA Cup:
Arsenal 2
Sheffield Wednesday 1 (replay aet)

League Cup:
Arsenal 2
Sheffield Wednesday 1

Champions League:
Marseille 1 AC Milan 0

Scottish Premier:
Rangers

THE £300 MILLION KICK-OFF

The 22 founding members of the Premier League included Leeds United, the reigning Division One champions.

The Elland Road side had lifted the top-flight under boss Howard Wilkinson – still the last Englishman to win the title.

Luton, Notts County and West Ham missed out on the chance of taking part in the new competition as they had been relegated from Division One.

Ipswich and Middlesbrough were promoted from the old Second Division, along with Blackburn who won that division's play-off final.

The other founders were the rest of the teams from Division One, who had broken away from League Football and won a £300m-plus television deal from BSkyB and the BBC.

Brian Deane scored the Premiership's first-ever goal as Manchester United lost 2-1 to Sheffield United on opening day.

But with Eric Cantona signing from Leeds that November the Red Devils bounced back to win their eighth league title.

TOP SCORER

Teddy Sheringham was the top scorer with 22 for Tottenham. He had joined Spurs from Nottingham Forest for £2.1m, having scored Forest's first goal in the new division, in a 1-1 with Liverpool. Just a week after that goal he was heading south.

TOP TRANSFER

The 21-year-old Alan Shearer was sold from Southampton to Blackburn for a then British record £3.5m. After four years with Saints and 43 goals in 158 games, he turned down Manchester United in favour of Rovers and their boss Kenny Dalglish.

BARCLAYS PREMIER LEAGUE

1992-93

IT'S A FACT

PFA Player of the Year was Man United's Eric Cantona who had weighed in with 25 goals to help his side clinch the Double. United were then only the fourth side that century to win both the League and FA Cup in the same year, after Spurs, Arsenal and Liverpool

FINAL TABLE

	P	GD	PTS
Manchester United	42	42	92
Blackburn	42	27	84
Newcastle	42	41	77
Arsenal	42	25	71
Leeds	42	26	70
Wimbledon	42	3	65
Sheff Wed	42	22	64
Liverpool	42	4	60
QPR	42	1	60
Aston Villa	42	-4	57
Coventry	42	-2	56
Norwich	42	4	53
West Ham	42	-11	52
Chelsea	42	-4	51
Tottenham	42	-5	45
Manchester City	42	-11	45
Everton	42	-21	44
Southampton	42	-17	43
Ipswich	42	-23	43
Sheffield United	42	-18	42
Oldham	42	-26	40
Swindon	42	-53	30

ELSEWHERE...

FA Cup:
Man United 4 Chelsea 0

League Cup:
Aston Villa 3 Man United 1

Champions League:
AC Milan 4 Barcelona 0

Scottish Premier:
Rangers

ROVERS AND OUT...

Manchester United retained the title – but there was a period when it looked like they might just throw it away.

Blackburn were 16 points behind the leaders at the turn of the year but capitalised as United went through a bumpy patch.

When the two sides met and Rovers won that game the gap went down to just three points.

But in the end the reigning champions had eight points to spare over the side who were spending a lot of owner Jack Walker's cash in search of silverware.

There was also drama at the foot of the table where Everton looked like losing their ever-present status in England's top-flight until victory on the final day.

Sheffield United looked safe a number of places above the relegation spots going into the final day but they were beaten by a last-minute goal from Chelsea and went down with Oldham and Swindon.

Swindon disappeared with a record they didn't want, having won just five games all season, conceding 100 goals in the process.

TOP SCORER

Andy Cole hit an amazing tally of 34 – still a best for the league – as newly promoted Newcastle United, under Kevin Keegan, stamped their arrival on the division. Cole the Goal hit seven more in all competitions!

TOP TRANSFER

Republic of Ireland star Roy Keane left Nottingham Forest to join Manchester United in a £3.75m move. It was a record deal for an English club and Keano would have a tremendous impact on the future of the Red Devils.

IT'S A FACT

Newcastle United boss Kevin Keegan won two of the nine Manager of the Month awards, the only boss to win more than one that season.

FINAL TABLE

	P	GD	PTS
Blackburn	42	41	89
Manchester United	42	49	88
Nottingham Forest	42	29	77
Liverpool	42	28	74
Leeds	42	21	73
Newcastle	42	20	72
Tottenham	42	8	62
QPR	42	2	60
Wimbledon	42	-17	56
Southampton	42	-2	54
Chelsea	42	-5	54
Arsenal	42	3	51
Sheff Wed	42	-8	51
West Ham	42	-4	50
Everton	42	-7	50
Coventry	42	-18	50
Manchester City	42	-11	49
Aston Villa	42	-5	48
Crystal Palace	42	-15	45
Norwich	42	-17	43
Leicester	42	-35	29
Ipswich	42	-57	27

ELSEWHERE...

FA Cup:
Everton 1 Man United 0

League Cup:
Liverpool 2 Bolton 1

Champions League:
Ajax 1 AC Milan 0

Scottish Premier:
Rangers

BLACKBURN ARE BEST

Big-spending Blackburn, who had already broken the British transfer record when they bought striker Alan Shearer, raised the stakes yet again.

They forked out £5m to Norwich City for hitman Chris Sutton to form the partnership that was to become known as the SAS.

Their spending certainly paid off as boss Kenny Dalglish's side broke Manchester United's monopoly of the Premier League.

This is the season that will not just be remembered for Rovers' title-win, but also for Eric Cantona's amazing kung-fu kick on a Crystal Palace fan.

Cantona jumped into the Selhurst Park crowd feet first as his side drew 1-1 and was later banned from football for eight months and fined £20,000. He was also ordered to do community service.

Promoted Nottingham Forest had gone into the season without legendary boss Brian Clough, but former defender Frank Clark took over at the City Ground and led them into third.

This was also the year when "diving" entered into the English game. German Jurgen Klinsmann, signed by Tottenham, even ridiculed the allegations made against him by performing a dive across the pitch when he scored.

TOP SCORER

Alan Shearer's boots helped fire Blackburn to the top with 34 goals. Sutton hit a further 15 goals for the Ewood Park side.

TOP TRANSFER

Although Chris Sutton had set a new best, yet another British record was created when Newcastle agreed to sell striker Andy Cole to Manchester United for £6m. Winger Keith Gillespie went in the opposite direction as part of the deal.

BARCLAYS PREMIER LEAGUE

1994-95

IT'S A FACT

Les Ferdinand, who had joined Newcastle from QPR for £6m, was voted the PFA Players' Player of the Year. He was the division's third-top scorer with 25, behind Alan Shearer and Robbie Fowler. Fowler was Young Player of the Year for a second successive season.

FINAL TABLE

	P	GD	PTS
Man United	38	38	82
Newcastle United	38	29	78
Liverpool	38	36	71
Aston Villa	38	17	63
Arsenal	38	17	63
Everton	38	20	61
Blackburn	38	14	61
Tottenham	38	12	61
Nott'm Forest	38	-4	58
West Ham	38	-9	51
Chelsea	38	2	50
Middlesbrough	38	-15	43
Leeds	38	-17	43
Wimbledon	38	-15	41
Sheff Wed	38	-13	40
Coventry	38	-18	38
Southampton	38	-18	38
Man City	38	-25	38
QPR	38	-19	33
Bolton	38	-32	29

ELSEWHERE...

FA Cup:
Man United 1 Liverpool 0

League Cup:
Aston Villa 3 Leeds 0

Champions League:
Juventus 1 Ajax 1
(Juve 4-2 on pens)

Scottish Premier:
Rangers

DOUBLE TOP FOR THE RED DEVILS!

The Premier League dropped its numbers down to 20 teams – Manchester United still completed the Double.

Only two sides came up from the second flight, champions Middlesbrough and play-off winners Bolton, but it was a team promoted the previous year that was the one to watch.

Newcastle United, third in their first Premier League season, were 12 points clear in January but by early March they were a single point ahead of the other United.

Newcastle dominated their home fixture against the Red Devils but lost 1-0 to an Eric Cantona goal and it was the beginning of the end of their title dreams.

Newcastle boss Kevin Keegan, Man United gaffer Sir Alex Ferguson and Liverpool chief Roy Evans all lifted two Manager of the Month awards.

Bolton's 15-year exile from the top-flight lasted just one season as they went straight back down, whilst Manchester City suffered relegation on goal difference, after seven years in the top tier.

TOP SCORER

Alan Shearer was the league's top scorer for the second successive season. His total of 31 for Blackburn was just three behind the strikes he had made the previous campaign.

TOP TRANSFER

Liverpool forked out £8.4m to Nottingham Forest for striker Stan Collymore.

But Newcastle United also set a new best for a defender when they paid Wimbledon £4m for full back Warren Barton.

IT'S A FACT

Manchester United's French forward Eric Cantona retired from the game. He had cost them just £1.5m and was the catalyst that kick-started their dominance of the league for so many years.

FINAL TABLE

	P	GD	PTS
Manchester United	38	32	75
Newcastle	38	33	68
Arsenal	38	30	68
Liverpool	38	25	68
Aston Villa	38	13	61
Chelsea	38	3	59
Sheff Wed	38	-1	57
Wimbledon	38	3	56
Leicester	38	-8	47
Tottenham	38	-7	46
Leeds	38	-10	46
Derby	38	-13	46
Blackburn	38	-1	42
West Ham	38	-9	42
Everton	38	-13	42
Southampton	38	-6	41
Coventry	38	-16	41
Sunderland	38	-18	40
Middlesbrough	38	-9	39
Nott'm Forest	38	-28	34

ELSEWHERE...

FA Cup:
Chelsea 2 Middlesbrough 0

League Cup:
Leicester 1 Middlesbrough 0
(replay)

Champions League:
Borussia Dortmund 3
Juventus 1

Scottish Premier:
Rangers

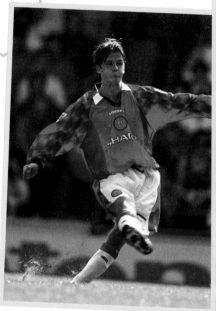

SEASON OF SHOCKS

An amazing goal, two humiliating defeats for Manchester United, a controversial relegation and yet another world record transfer (see below) made this a season to remember.

David Beckham scored from the half way line for United against Wimbledon on the opening day – a strike which was later voted Goal of the Decade.

His side were later thrashed 5-0 at Newcastle, their heaviest defeat in 12 years. In their next match, Manchester United were hit by a 6-3 humiliation at Southampton.

The Red Devils still won the league, their 11th title in total, having enjoyed a run of 16 games unbeaten.

Arsenal welcomed manager Arsene Wenger and midfielder Patrick Vieira but missed out on a European Cup place.

At the other end of the table Middlesbrough went down on the final day of the season, having suffered a points deduction for failing to play a game in December when they claimed their squad had been decimated by illness.

If they hadn't lost those three points Boro would have stayed up. Instead they went down with Sunderland and Nottingham Forest.

TOP SCORER

Shearer immediately paid off a huge chunk of his transfer fee with 25 Premier League goals as he helped the Geordies to runner-up spot. Arsenal's Ian Wright scored 23 league goals.

TOP TRANSFER

The £15m Newcastle forked out to take local hero Alan Shearer from Blackburn Rovers set a new world record. The England striker turned down Manchester United for his home-town club.

BARCLAYS PREMIER LEAGUE

1996-97

IT'S A FACT

Barnsley's one season stay in the top-flight after a 102-year wait included a 7-0 defeat at Manchester United and 6-0 at West Ham. But they gained some revenge by knocking United out of the FA Cup.

FINAL TABLE

	P	GD	PTS
Arsenal	38	35	78
Man United	38	47	77
Liverpool	38	26	65
Chelsea	38	28	63
Leeds	38	11	59
Blackburn	38	5	58
Aston Villa	38	1	57
West Ham	38	-1	56
Derby	38	3	55
Leicester	38	10	53
Coventry	38	2	52
Southampton	38	-5	48
Newcastle	38	-9	44
Tottenham	38	-12	44
Wimbledon	38	-12	44
Sheff Wed	38	-15	44
Everton	38	-15	40
Bolton	38	-20	40
Barnsley	38	-45	35
Crystal Palace	38	-34	33

ELSEWHERE...

FA Cup:
Arsenal 2 Newcastle 0

League Cup:
Chelsea 2 Middlesbrough 0

Champions League:
Real Madrid 1 Juventus 0

Scottish Premier:
Celtic

MAKE MINE A DOUBLE DOUBLE!

Arsenal became only the second team to complete a League and FA Cup Double for a second time.

The Gunners had last achieved the Double in 1971 and in Arsene Wenger's first full season in charge they equalled Manchester United's achievement for a second time.

Ironically, United had been 11 points ahead of the Gunners at one stage and some bookies even paid out cash to punters who had bet on Fergie's men retaining the title!

The Frenchman became the first overseas boss ever to win the top-flight in England and only the third boss, after Scots Sir Alex Ferguson and Kenny Dalglish, to lift the Premier League.

Wenger was Manager of the Year whilst his Dutch forward Dennis Bergkamp was both PFA and Football Writers' Footballer of the Year. Striker Ian Wright became the club's record goalscorer.

Derby and Bolton set up home in their new stadiums but it was not a happy season for Wanderers, relegated under Colin Todd. The three promoted sides from the previous season all went back down.

TOP SCORER

Three players were joint top scorers after a season that had produced more than 1,000 goals. There were 18 each for Coventry's Dion Dublin, Liverpool's Michael Owen, the PFA Young Player of the Year, and Chris Sutton of Blackburn Rovers.

TOP TRANSFER

Sheffield Wednesday forked out almost £4m to buy Italian striker Paolo Di Canio from Celtic. His first season produced 14 goals, 12 in the league. Teddy Sheringham left Tottenham for Manchester United.

19 YEARS OF THE PREMIER LEAGUE

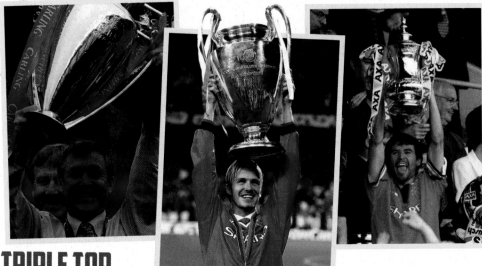

IT'S A FACT

Blackburn Rovers became the first side to have won the Premier League and to be relegated from the division. Boss Roy Hodgson was sacked almost four months into the season and replacement Brian Kidd couldn't keep them up.

FINAL TABLE

	P	GD	PTS
Manchester United	38	43	79
Arsenal	38	42	78
Chelsea	38	27	75
Leeds	38	28	67
West Ham	38	-7	57
Aston Villa	38	5	55
Liverpool	38	19	54
Derby	38	-5	52
Middlesbrough	38	-6	51
Leicester	38	-6	49
Tottenham	38	-3	47
Sheff Wed	38	-1	46
Newcastle	38	-6	46
Everton	38	-5	43
Coventry	38	-12	42
Wimbledon	38	-23	42
Southampton	38	-27	41
Charlton	38	-15	36
Blackburn	38	-14	35
Nott'm Forest	38	-34	30

ELSEWHERE...

FA Cup:
Man Utd 2 Newcastle Utd 0

League Cup:
Tottenham 1 Leicester City 0

Champions League:
Man Utd 2 Bayern Munich 1

Scottish Premier:
Rangers

TRIPLE TOP

Manchester United went on a £28m summer spending spree for Dwight Yorke, Jaap Stam and Jesper Blomqvist and recaptured the title from Arsenal.

The Gunners let in just 17 goals all season – the same number that top scorer Nicolas Anelka hit for them at the other end. The Frenchman was sold to Real Madrid at the end of the campaign.

United would go on to complete a Treble of the League, FA Cup and European Cup. Their Premier League win was completed on the final day of the season when they beat Spurs.

Ironically, Arsenal had beaten United in the Community Shield and 3-0 in the league at Highbury.

It was also the year when Arsenal brought in Kanu and sold Ian Wright; Villa bought Paul Merson and Dion Dublin; Chelsea signed Marcel Desailly; Liverpool appointed Gerard Houllier as boss and gave a contract to Steven Gerrard. Duncan Ferguson moved from Everton to Newcastle United.

Forest went down for a third time in seven seasons, Ron Atkinson replaced Dave Bassett as manager but still took just seven wins all season and suffered a humiliating 8-1 home defeat to Man United.

TOP SCORER

Once again three players all scored 18 goals to be joint top scorers: Jimmy Floyd Hasselbaink of Leeds, Liverpool's Michael Owen and Man United's Dwight Yorke.

TOP TRANSFER

Sir Alex Ferguson smashed the Manchester United transfer record twice by signing Dwight Yorke from Villa for £12.6m and Jaap Stam for £10.6m. He also paid £9.4m for Jesper Blomqvist. Wimbledon set a new club best when they gave West Ham United £7.5m for striker John Hartson.

1998-99

SHOOT'S ULTIMATE BOOK OF FOOTBALL 2012

IT'S A FACT

Alan Shearer may have been knocked off his top-scorer's perch but he hit FIVE in Newcastle's 8-0 demolition of Sheffield Wednesday. It was Sir Bobby Robson's first home game in charge of the Toon.

FINAL TABLE

	P	GD	PTS
Man United	38	52	91
Arsenal	38	30	73
Leeds	38	15	69
Liverpool	38	21	67
Chelsea	38	19	65
Aston Villa	38	11	58
Sunderland	38	1	58
Leicester	38	0	55
West Ham	38	-1	55
Tottenham	38	8	53
Newcastle	38	9	52
Middlesbrough	38	-6	52
Everton	38	10	50
Coventry	38	-7	44
Southampton	38	-17	44
Derby	38	-13	38
Bradford City	38	-30	36
Wimbledon	38	-28	33
Sheff Wed	38	-32	31
Watford	38	-42	24

ELSEWHERE...

FA Cup:
Chelsea 2 Aston Villa 0

League Cup:
Leicester 2 Tranmere 1

Champions League:
Real Madrid 3 Valencia 0

Scottish Premier:
Rangers

FERGIE'S FLYING!

Sir Alex Ferguson picked up three of the nine Manager of the Month awards as Manchester United retained the title.

The Red Devils were a staggering 18 points clear of nearest rivals Arsenal and lost just three games all season as they collected their sixth Premier League trophy.

But in a season when the old Wembley was shutting its gates for the final time, there was controversy when United were allowed to miss the FA Cup so that they could compete in the World Club Championships.

Sir Bobby Robson became the oldest manager in the division's history at the age of 66 when he took over at Newcastle United, the club he had supported as a boy.

Bradford City were back in the top-flight for the first time in 77 years and stayed up thanks to a 1-0 victory over Liverpool on the final day of the season, David Wetherall scoring.

Watford, with former England gaffer Graham Taylor back in charge, finished rock bottom with a new Premier League low of just 24 points.

Going down with them were Wimbledon, who had taken just nine years to get to the top of the football pyramid having only entered the Football League in 1977.

TOP SCORER

Sunderland's Kevin Phillips smashed in 30 goals, top-scoring in the Premier League, and won the European Golden Boot.

TOP TRANSFER

Arsenal paid a club record £11m to Juventus for Thierry Henry and Chelsea forked out £10m to buy Blackburn striker Chris Sutton.

19 YEARS OF THE PREMIER L

IT'S A FACT

Three bosses were in charge of Bradford City this season. Paul Jewell had his resignation refused before the kick-off. Assistant Chris Hutchings took over for 21 games before getting the sack in November 2000. He was replaced by Jim Jefferies from Hearts.

FINAL TABLE

	P	GD	PTS
Man United	38	48	80
Arsenal	38	25	70
Liverpool	38	32	69
Leeds	38	21	68
Ipswich	38	15	66
Chelsea	38	23	61
Sunderland	38	5	57
Aston Villa	38	3	54
Charlton	38	-7	52
Southampton	38	-8	52
Newcastle	38	-6	51
Tottenham	38	-7	49
Leicester	38	-12	48
Middlesbrough	38	0	42
West Ham	38	-5	42
Everton	38	-14	42
Derby	38	-22	42
Man City	38	-24	34
Coventry	38	-27	34
Bradford City	38	-40	26

ELSEWHERE...

FA Cup:
Liverpool 2 Arsenal 1

League Cup:
Liverpool 1 Birmingham City 1
(Liverpool 5-4 on pens)

Champions League:
Bayern Munich 1 Valencia 1
(Bayern 5-4 on pens)

Scottish Premier: Celtic

SO THREESY...

Manchester United won their third title in a row – to give yet another record to Sir Alex Ferguson. The Scot became the first manager to win three successive top-flight English titles.

Arsenal were once again the bridesmaids as they reached three seasons without silverware.

More than half of the 20 teams changed their managers, including Chelsea who departed company with Gianluca Vialli. He had won five trophies during less than two years in charge.

Liverpool climbed to third but it was the three trophies won by boss Gerard Houllier – League, FA and UEFA Cups – plus the crowning of Steven Gerrard as PFA Young Player of the Year that had Anfield celebrating.

There had been returns to the Premier League for Charlton, Ipswich and Manchester City. The Tractor Boys celebrated in style by qualifying for the UEFA Cup and boss George Burley was named by his fellow gaffers as Manager of the Year.

Southampton ended their 103-year stay at The Dell, legendary midfielder Matt Le Tissier scoring the final goal at the ground on the final day of the season.

Man City went straight back down having been away for four years. Coventry City were also relegated after 34 consecutive seasons in the top-flight.

TOP SCORER

Former Leeds star Hasselbaink marked his return to English football with 23 goals for Chelsea. Ipswich's Marcus Stewart scored 19 times.

TOP TRANSFER

Chelsea began the season with the record equalling buy of £15m Jimmy Floyd Hasselbaink from Atletico Madrid. Leeds forked out £18m, to buy Rio Ferdinand from West Ham.

BARCLAYS PREMIER LEAGUE

2000-01

GUNNERS SHOOT BACK TO THE TOP

Arsenal finally broke Manchester United's domination to claim their second Premier League title.

The Gunners completed their third league and cup Double, their second under French boss Arsene Wenger, who agreed a new deal with the club as veteran defenders Tony Adams and Lee Dixon called time on their careers.

Ironically, it was a win at Old Trafford in the penultimate game of the campaign that clinched the title for the North Londoners. A draw would have been good enough but Sylvain Wiltord got the only goal of the game.

Big-spending United had to settle for third behind Liverpool and just two wins ahead of Newcastle who had also been in the title race with the top three.

Chelsea couldn't string together a decent run of form under Claudio Ranieri who had brought in £11m midfielder Frank Lampard from West Ham plus £7.5m winger Bolo Zenden from Barcelona. Veteran skipper Denis Wise was sold and Gus Poyet allowed to leave.

Fulham returned to the top-flight after a 33-year gap and spent £34m of players, including £11.5m on striker Steve Marlet, a club record.

Sir Alex Ferguson had announced his retirement from Manchester United at the end of the season… it never happened!

IT'S A FACT

For the first time, all of the promoted teams retained their Premier League status. Fulham, Bolton and Blackburn Rovers all avoided the dreaded drop.

FINAL TABLE

	P	GD	PTS
Arsenal	38	43	87
Liverpool	38	37	80
Man United	38	42	77
Newcastle	38	22	71
Leeds	38	16	66
Chelsea	38	28	64
West Ham	38	-9	53
Aston Villa	38	-1	50
Tottenham	38	-4	50
Blackburn	38	4	46
Southampton	38	-8	45
Middlesbrough	38	-12	45
Fulham	38	-8	44
Charlton	38	-11	44
Everton	38	-12	43
Bolton	38	-18	40
Sunderland	38	-22	40
Ipswich	38	-23	36
Derby	38	-30	30
Leicester	38	-34	28

ELSEWHERE...

FA Cup:
Arsenal 2 Chelsea 0

League Cup:
Blackburn 2 Tottenham 1

Champions League:
Real Madrid 2
Bayer Leverkusen 1

Scottish Premier:
Celtic

TOP SCORER

Arsene Wenger converted speedy and tricky winger Thierry Henry into a striker and was rewarded with a table-topping 24 goals. That was one more than Chelsea's Jimmy Floyd Hasselbaink, Newcastle United's Alan Shearer and Manchester United new boy Ruud van Nistelrooy

TOP TRANSFER

Man United spent heavily, with £19m to PSV Eindhoven for Holland striker Ruud van Nistelrooy and a staggering £28.1m to Lazio for Argentina midfielder Juan Sebastian Veron. Robbie Fowler left Liverpool for Leeds United in an £11m deal.

IT'S A FACT

Arsenal's France striker Thierry Henry hit 24 league goals and lifted the PFA Players' Player of the Year award. He also won Goal of the Season for a strike against Tottenham.

FINAL TABLE

	P	GD	PTS
Man United	38	40	83
Arsenal	38	43	78
Newcastle	38	15	69
Chelsea	38	30	67
Liverpool	38	20	64
Blackburn	38	9	60
Everton	38	-1	59
Southampton	38	-3	52
Man City	38	-7	51
Tottenham	38	-11	50
Middlesbrough	38	4	49
Charlton	38	-11	49
Birmingham	38	-8	48
Fulham	38	-9	48
Leeds	38	1	47
Aston Villa	38	-5	45
Bolton	38	-10	44
West Ham	38	-17	42
West Brom	38	-36	26
Sunderland	38	-44	19

ELSEWHERE...

FA Cup:
Arsenal 1 Southampton 0

League Cup:
Liverpool 2 Man United 0

Champions League:
AC Milan 0 Juventus 0
(Milan 3-2 on pens)

Scottish Premier:
Rangers

RECORDS CRASH

Rio Ferdinand set a new world transfer record when he moved from Leeds to Manchester United for £30m.

He helped United to take the title back from Arsenal despite David Beckham departing from Old Trafford as he arrived.

Ironically, it was Ferdinand's former club's shock away victory against the Gunners that ensured the title headed to Old Trafford.

Another record crashed at the foot of the table as Sunderland amassed just 19 points, then the lowest in Premier League history. They sacked both Peter Reid and Howard Wilkinson before appointing Mick McCarthy as manager.

Leeds sacked boss David O'Leary and appointed former England coach Terry Venables as manager. Despite the cash collected from selling Ferdinand, he took over at a club crippled by debt after heavy spending on players.

Chelsea landed their first crack at the Champions League in four years and were set up for the following season by the arrival of new billionaire owner Roman Abramovich.

Two wins in 21 games saw Bolton needing to win on the final day to stay up, something they managed with a 2-1 victory. And Liverpool also went on a terrible run with just two wins in 16, after a start of 12 games unbeaten!

Gordon Strachan took Southampton to the FA Cup Final and eighth, their best-ever Premier League finish to date.

TOP SCORER

The Golden Boot went to Man United's Dutch striker Ruud van Nistelrooy with 25 league goals, and 44 in total. He was also named Barclaycard Player of the Year. He had one more league goal than Arsenal's Thierry Henry.

TOP TRANSFER

Besides the Ferdinand move there was a £13m switch from Liverpool to Man City for striker Nicolas Anelka as Anfield recruited £10m Senegal hitman El-Hadji Diouf.

BARCLAYS PREMIER LEAGUE

2002-03

IT'S A FACT

Arsenal striker Thierry Henry was the PFA Players' Player of the Year for a second successive season. The Frenchman also added two Player of the Month awards, was voted Fans' Player of the Year and Football Writers' Footballer of the Year.

FINAL TABLE

	P	GD	PTS
Arsenal	38	47	90
Chelsea	38	37	79
Man United	38	29	75
Liverpool	38	18	60
Newcastle	38	12	56
Aston Villa	38	4	56
Charlton	38	0	53
Bolton	38	-8	53
Fulham	38	6	52
Birmingham	38	-5	50
Middlesbrough	38	-8	48
Southampton	38	-1	47
Portsmouth	38	-7	45
Tottenham	38	-10	45
Blackburn	38	-8	44
Man City	38	1	41
Everton	38	-12	39
Leicester	38	-17	33
Leeds	38	-39	33
Wolves	38	-39	33

ELSEWHERE...

FA Cup:
Man United 3 Millwall 0

League Cup:
Middlesbrough 2 Bolton 1

Champions League:
Porto 3 Monaco 0

Scottish Premier:
Celtic

SALUTE THE INVINCIBLES!

Arsene Wenger made history, as he became the first manager to lift the LMA Manager of the Year twice as he guided Arsenal to an unbeaten season.

The Gunners took the title back from Man United with 26 wins and 12 draws as their impressive side earned the nickname of The Invincibles. Backed by the midfield strength of Patrick Vieira and the tricky wing play of Robert Pires, Thierry Henry shone like a beacon as Arsenal became only the second team ever to go through a league programme unbeaten.

Wenger won two Manager of the Month awards – the same total as Sam Allardyce who took Bolton to eighth, their best finish in 50 years.

Chelsea began their big-spending under new owner Abramovich who parted with £100m for players, which included the impressive Claude Makelele. Runner-up spot was not good enough to save boss Claudio Ranieri. Leeds were also £100m worse off – but their crippling debts led to the sale of major players and relegation.

As Fulham appointed the top-flight's youngster-ever manager in the form of Chris Coleman, Liverpool sacked Gerard Houllier, despite his success with trophies and finishing fourth, yet again.

Ruud van Nistelrooy hit another 30 goals for Man United, 20 in the league, but third place was a bitter disappointment for the Red Devils.

Portsmouth's debut season saw them as the only survivors among the promoted sides. Leicester were down before the final day and Wolves failure to win an away game saw them relegated.

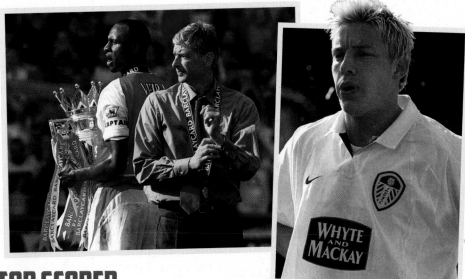

TOP SCORER

Thierry Henry went one better than the previous season, finishing top of the scoring charts. His 30 league strikes for Arsenal was eight more than Alan Shearer's total.

TOP TRANSFER

Cristiano Ronaldo arrived at Man United for £12m and pulled on the No.7 shirt vacated by David Beckham. He scored six goals in his first Old Trafford campaign, including one in United's FA Cup victory.

IT'S A FACT

PFA Player of the Year was Chelsea's title-winning captain John Terry but the Fans' Player of the Year was his friend and team-mate Frank Lampard. Blues boss Mourinho was Manager of the Season.

FINAL TABLE

	P	GD	PTS
Chelsea	38	57	95
Arsenal	38	51	83
Man United	38	32	77
Everton	38	-1	61
Liverpool	38	11	58
Bolton	38	5	58
Middlesbrough	38	7	55
Man City	38	8	52
Tottenham	38	6	52
Aston Villa	38	-7	47
Charlton	38	-16	46
Birmingham	38	-6	45
Fulham	38	-8	44
Newcastle	38	-10	44
Blackburn	38	-11	42
Portsmouth	38	-16	39
West Brom	38	-25	34
Crystal Palace	38	-21	33
Norwich	38	-35	33
Southampton	38	-21	32

ELSEWHERE...

FA Cup:
Arsenal 0 Man United 0
(Arsenal 5-4 on pens)

League Cup:
Chelsea 3 Liverpool 2 (aet)

Champions League:
Liverpool 3 AC Milan 3
(Liverpool 3-2 on pens)

Scottish Premier:
Rangers

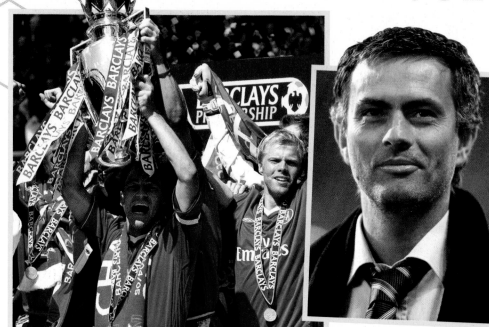

BLUE IS THE COLOUR!

Chelsea lifted their first top-flight title in 50 years to smash the Manchester United and Arsenal domination of the Premier League.

It was only the second title win by the Blues and heralded the arrival of Jose Mourinho, who dubbed himself The Special One at his first press conference. The Portugal-born manager's side finished 12 points clear of deposed champions Arsenal and he added the League Cup for good measure.

Their 95-point haul was a new record but it had cost the Blues an amazing £250m to assemble their side. Other records tumbled as Chelsea had the most victories and fewest goals conceded. Keeper Petr Cech kept ten clean sheets.

Manchester City were the only side to beat Chelsea.

Newcastle surprisingly axed Sir Bobby Robson as manager and appointed Graeme Souness who had left Blackburn. The Geordies slumped to 14th after the relative success of previous seasons.

Promoted West Brom clung on to survival but fellow promoted sides Crystal Palace and Norwich City went straight back down Southampton disappeared after 27 years in the top-flight.

TOP SCORER

Thierry Henry won the Golden Boot for a third time as he hit 25 goals for Arsenal. That was four goals more than Andy Johnson of Crystal Palace.

TOP TRANSFER

Eighteen-year-old Wayne Rooney arrived at Manchester United for a staggering £25.6m after the Red Devils won a bidding war with Newcastle. He scored a hat-trick on his debut, against Fenerbahce in the Champions League and was named Football Writers' Footballer of the Year.

BARCLAYS PREMIER LEAGUE

2004-05

IT'S A FACT

Steven Gerrard was the PFA Players' Player of the Year, beating fellow Scouser Wayne Rooney who did win the Young Player of the Year award and was voted as the fans' No.1 too.

FINAL TABLE

	P	GD	PTS
Chelsea	38	50	91
Man United	38	38	83
Liverpool	38	32	82
Arsenal	38	37	67
Tottenham	38	15	65
Blackburn	38	9	63
Newcastle	38	5	58
Bolton	38	8	56
West Ham	38	-3	55
Wigan	38	-7	51
Everton	38	-15	50
Fulham	38	-10	48
Charlton	38	-14	47
Middlesbrough	38	-10	45
Man City	38	-5	43
Aston Villa	38	-13	42
Portsmouth	38	-25	38
Birmingham	38	-22	34
West Brom	38	-27	30
Sunderland	38	-43	15

ELSEWHERE...

FA Cup:
Liverpool 3 West Ham 3
(Liverpool 3-1 on pens)

League Cup:
Man United 4 Wigan 0

Champions League:
Barcelona 2 Arsenal 1

Scottish Premier:
Celtic

DOUBLE TOP!

Chelsea completed back-to-back titles under Jose Mourinho – holding off a late surge from Manchester United. The Blues got off to a blistering start with 15 wins in 16 games and at one point were an incredible 18 points ahead of their nearest challengers.

United's challenge was over when they were beaten at Chelsea 3-0 and relegation threatened Sunderland drew at Old Trafford.

Rock bottom Sunderland would end the season with just 15 points, four less than when they set the previous worst. It meant a return to the Championship after just one season.

Paul Jewell, boss of newly promoted Wigan, collected two Manager of the Month awards as he steered his side to safety. The same number of awards was collected by Rafa Benitez at Liverpool whose side recorded the highest total of points for a team finishing third.

West Brom went down having failed to pull off a miracle escape like they had the previous season.

The biggest drama at the end of the season left Tottenham players feeling doubly sick! Spurs looked to have a European place in the bag but the night before their crucial clash with West Ham a number of players were struck down with food poisoning and police took away samples amid fears of tampering! Spurs lost 2-1 and bitter rivals Arsenal got the European spot.

TOP SCORER

France ace Thierry Henry was yet again the league's top scorer, this time with 27. Three of those came in the last match ever at Highbury, before the Gunners moved to the Emirates Stadium, and helped him win the Football Writers' Footballer of the Year award for a record third time.

TOP TRANSFER

Holland keeper Edwin van der Sar moved from Fulham to Manchester United for what turned out to be a bargain £2m. Winger Shaun Wright-Phillips went from Manchester City to Chelsea for a staggering £21m, which turned out to be not such a good buy!

19 YEARS OF THE PREMIER LEAGUE

IT'S A FACT

Paul Robinson became only the third keeper – after Peter Schmeichel and Brad Friedel – to score a Premier League goal. His free-kick bounced over Ben Foster to give Spurs a 3-1 victory at White Hart Lane. It was the first time a scoring keeper had been on the winning side.

FINAL TABLE

	P	GD	PTS
Man United	38	56	89
Chelsea	38	40	83
Liverpool	38	30	68
Arsenal	38	28	68
Tottenham	38	3	60
Everton	38	16	58
Bolton	38	-5	56
Reading	38	5	55
Portsmouth	38	3	54
Blackburn	38	-2	52
Aston Villa	38	2	50
Newcastle	38	-5	46
Middlesbrough	38	-9	43
Man City	38	-15	42
West Ham	38	-24	41
Fulham	38	-22	39
Wigan	38	-22	38
Sheffield United	38	-23	38
Charlton	38	-26	34
Watford	38	-30	28

ELSEWHERE...

FA Cup:
Chelsea 1 Man United 0 (aet)

League Cup:
Chelsea 2 Arsenal 1

Champions League:
AC Milan 2 Liverpool 1

Scottish Premier:
Celtic

UNITED FRONT FOR FERGIE'S MEN

After two years without the title Manchester United had the trophy back in the bag with two games still to play.

Chelsea, champions for the previous two seasons, were seven points off the pace heading into those two final fixtures after they failed to beat Arsenal at the new Emirates Stadium.

There was even more kudos for the Red Devils as boss Sir Alex Ferguson won three Manager of the Month awards and was voted Manager of the Season; Cristiano Ronaldo was the PFA Players' Player and Young Player of the Year and bagged 17 league goals in the process.

Reading were the surprise promotion package. Two down early in their first game, at home to Middlesbrough, they bounced back to win 3-2. They also recorded the biggest win of the season, thrashing West Ham 6-0 at the Madejski Stadium on their way to eighth.

Fulham conceded the most goals during this campaign – 60 – but the one scored by their defender Moritz Volz against Chelsea created a bit of history as it was the 15,000th in the Premier League.

Sheffield United and Watford had one season in the top-flight before instant relegation whilst Charlton dropped out after eight years.

TOP SCORER

Chelsea's Ivory Coast striker Didier Drogba, shortlisted for the PFA Player of the Year award, was leading marksman with 20 goals. That was two more than Blackburn's Benni McCarthy.

TOP TRANSFER

Ukraine striker Andriy Shevchenko arrived at Chelsea from AC Milan for a staggering £30.8m, along with £9m Salomon Kalou from Feyenoord and £16m John Obi Mikel from Lyn Oslo. Dimitar Berbatov was a £10.9m buy for Tottenham from Bayer Leverkusen.

BARCLAYS PREMIER LEAGUE

2006-07

IT'S A FACT

The biggest victory of the season was Middlesbrough's staggering 8-1 home win over Manchester City. But Portsmouth's 7-4 win over Reading was the biggest aggregate score in Premier League history.

FINAL TABLE

	P	GD	PTS
Man United	38	58	87
Chelsea	38	39	85
Arsenal	38	43	83
Liverpool	38	39	76
Everton	38	22	65
Aston Villa	38	20	60
Blackburn	38	2	58
Portsmouth	38	8	57
Man City	38	-8	55
West Ham	38	-8	49
Tottenham	38	5	46
Newcastle	38	-20	43
Middlesbrough	38	-10	42
Wigan	38	-17	40
Sunderland	38	-23	39
Bolton	38	-18	37
Fulham	38	-22	36
Reading	38	-25	36
Birmingham	38	-16	35
Derby	38	-69	11

ELSEWHERE...

FA Cup:
Portsmouth 1 Cardiff City 0

League Cup:
Tottenham 2 Chelsea 1 (aet)

Champions League:
Man United 1 Chelsea 1
(United 6-5 on pens)

Scottish Premier:
Celtic

RONNIE'S FINEST HOUR

The same big four clubs battled it out for the title of champions but it was once again Manchester United who clinched the trophy.

The victory took them to 17 top-flight titles, just one off Liverpool's all-time record. United were heavily aided by the scintillating form of Portugal winger Cristiano Ronaldo who mesmerised defenders with his step-overs and lethal shooting.

He won the PFA Players' Player of the Year award and Barclays Player of the Season for a second successive year, lifted the same title from the fans and was also Football Writers' Footballer of the Year.

Sir Alex Ferguson was Manager of the Season for an eighth time. There was still no silverware for Arsenal, although Cesc Fabregas was named PFA Young Player of the Year.

At the opposite end of the table Derby took over as the Premier League's worst-ever points scorers with just 11, that included only one win.

It was also a memorable season for history making hat-tricks. Emmanuel Adebayor scored one both home and away for Arsenal against Wigan. Marcus Bent and Roque Santa Cruz each scored three in Wigan's 5-3 victory over Blackburn Rovers.

TOP SCORER

Cristiano Ronaldo pulled on the Golden Boot after 31 Premier League goals, seven more than both Liverpool's Fernando Torres and Emmanuel Adebayor of Arsenal. Ronnie totalled an amazing 42 goals in all competitions.

TOP TRANSFER

Man United boosted their squad with the arrival of Anderson from Porto for £17m, Nani from Sporting Lisbon for £14m and £17m Owen Hargreaves from Bayern Munich, and added Carlos Tevez. Liverpool took Ryan Babel from Ajax for £11.5m and paid Atletico Madrid £21.5m for Fernando Torres. Florent Malouda arrived at Chelsea from Lyon for £13.5m and Arsenal bought Dinamo Zagreb's Eduardo for £10m.

19 YEARS OF THE PREMIER LEAGUE

IT'S A FACT

Ryan Giggs was the PFA Players' Player of the Year and the Young Player of the Year was Aston Villa's Ashley Young. Steven Gerrard was Football Writers' Footballer of the Year.

FINAL TABLE

	P	GD	PTS
Man United	38	44	90
Liverpool	38	50	86
Chelsea	38	44	83
Arsenal	38	31	72
Everton	38	18	63
Aston Villa	38	6	62
Fulham	38	5	53
Tottenham	38	0	51
West Ham	38	-3	51
Man City	38	8	50
Wigan	38	-11	45
Stoke	38	-17	45
Bolton	38	-12	41
Portsmouth	38	-19	41
Blackburn	38	-20	41
Sunderland	38	-20	36
Hull	38	-25	35
Newcastle	38	-19	34
Middlesbrough	38	-29	32
West Brom	38	-31	32

ELSEWHERE...

FA Cup:
Chelsea 2 Everton 1

League Cup:
Man United 0 Tottenham 0
(United 4-1 on pens)

Champions League:
Barcelona 2 Man United 0

Scottish Premier:
Rangers

TALE OF TWO MANCHESTERS

This was the year Manchester City became one of the world's richest clubs – but it was their neighbours United who retained the title.

Old Trafford celebrated their eleventh Premier League crown as City counted the pound notes but still finished in tenth spot. As United's 18th top-flight victory it made them joint record holders with Liverpool for the most titles won in England.

New boy Robinho hit 14 league goals during his first term with City, who also had the biggest win of the season, 6-0 against Portsmouth.

Arsenal were involved in two 4-4 draws, one in the derby with Tottenham and the other at Liverpool where Andriy Arshavin hit all of their goals.

Despite the goal glut it was also a season remembered for goalkeeping firsts. Man United's Edwin van der Sar earned the Golden Glove for 21 clean sheets in 33 league appearances, including a record 11 games in a row.

Aston Villa keeper Brad Friedel got a Barclays award for appearing in 167 consecutive games and Portsmouth's David James broke the league's appearance record when he reached 536 games.

For the first time in three years more than one of the promoted teams stayed up, Hull City and Stoke City surviving.

West Brom were relegated before the final day.

Also down went Middlesbrough and Newcastle United, both with just seven wins, the fewest in the division.

Boro lost at West Ham whilst the Geordies failed to get the point they needed at Aston Villa, where Damien Duff's own goal cost them their status.

BARCLAYS PREMIER LEAGUE CHAMPIONS 2008-09

TOP SCORER

Chelsea's France striker Nicolas Anelka was top league scorer with 19 and won November's Player of the Month award. He was one goal ahead of Manchester United's Cristiano Ronaldo.

TOP TRANSFER

The British transfer record fell when Brazil striker Robinho joined Manchester City for a staggering £32.5m. The deal went through just seconds before the transfer window shut.

BARCLAYS PREMIER LEAGUE

2008-09

IT'S A FACT

Man United's Wayne Rooney was named as the PFA Players' Player of the Year and Football Writers' Footballer of the Year. Aston Villa's James Milner the Young Player of the Year and Harry Redknapp was LMA Manager of the Year.

FINAL TABLE

	P	GD	PTS
Chelsea	38	71	86
Man United	38	58	85
Arsenal	38	42	75
Tottenham	38	26	70
Man City	38	28	67
Aston Villa	38	13	64
Liverpool	38	26	63
Everton	38	11	61
Birmingham	38	-9	50
Blackburn	38	-14	50
Stoke	38	-14	47
Fulham	38	-7	46
Sunderland	38	-8	44
Bolton	38	-25	39
Wolves	38	-24	38
Wigan	38	-42	36
West Ham	38	-19	35
Burnley	38	-40	30
Hull	38	-41	30
Portsmouth	38	-32	19

ELSEWHERE...

FA Cup:
Chelsea 1 Portsmouth 0

League Cup:
Man United 2 Aston Villa 1

Champions League:
Inter Milan 2
Bayern Munich 0

Scottish Premier:
Rangers

KING CARLO OF THE BRIDGE

Carlo Ancelotti became king of Stamford Bridge, landing the League and FA Cup Double at the end of his first season in charge of Chelsea.

The Blues smashed home a Premier League record of 103 goals as they deposed Manchester United by one point and boasted the division's leading scorer.

It was the first time a team had hit more than 100 goals and beat the Premier League's previous best of 93 by Man United in 1999-00.

Chelsea also became the first team to score seven or more goals in four league games in one season. They hit eight against Wigan, seven against Sunderland, Stoke and Aston Villa.

The season got off to a sad start as players around the country stood in silent respect for former England, Ipswich Town and Newcastle United boss Sir Bobby Robson who passed away just two weeks before the kick-off.

There was joy for Spurs fans though when their side hit a season's best 9-1 victory over Wigan, Jermain Defoe getting five of the goals. They also qualified for the Champions League for the first time.

Portsmouth became the first team to go into administration since the formation of the Premiership and were deducted nine points. Their season hadn't got off to a great start with zero points after seven games and were the first team to be relegated. They were joined by Hull, who had only just avoided the drop the previous season. Burnley, back at the top level after 33 years, lasted just one season.

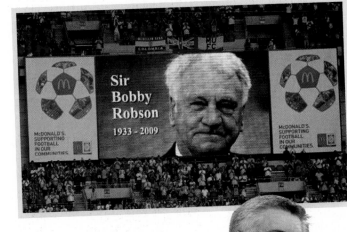

TOP SCORER

Chelsea's Ivory Coast striker Didier Drogba scored 29 goals to land the Golden Boot for a second time. He was three ahead of Man United's Wayne Rooney.

TOP TRANSFER

Man City went on a £117m spending spree for Carlos Tevez (£25m), Roque Santa Cruz (£18m), Kolo Toure (£15m), Emmanuel Adebayor (£25m), Joleon Lescott (£22m) and Gareth Barry (£12m).

IT'S A FACT

Tottenham and Wales star Gareth Bale was the PFA Players' Player of the Year for some amazing wing play. Arsenal and England's highly rated midfield prospect Jack Wilshere was Young Player of the Year.

FINAL TABLE

	P	GD	PTS
Man United	38	41	80
Chelsea	38	36	71
Man City	38	27	71
Arsenal	38	29	68
Tottenham	38	9	62
Liverpool	38	15	58
Everton	38	6	54
Fulham	38	6	49
Aston Villa	38	-11	48
Sunderland	38	-11	47
West Brom	38	-15	47
Newcastle	38	-1	46
Stoke	38	-2	46
Bolton	38	-4	46
Blackburn	38	-13	43
Wigan	38	-21	42
Wolves	38	-20	40
Birmingham	38	-21	39
Blackpool	38	-23	39
West Ham	38	-27	33

ELSEWHERE...

FA Cup:
Man City 1 Stoke City 0

League Cup:
Birmingham City 2 Arsenal 1

Champions League:
Barcelona 3 Man United 1

Scottish Premier:
Rangers

IT'S A RECORD!

Manchester United scored their 19th title win – the side's 12th in the Premier League – to set a new British record. Sir Alex Ferguson had been striving for years to beat Liverpool's record of 18 top-flight wins.

Although many pundits and fans reckoned this was not the best team Sir Alex had put together and was still a work in progress, the players proved otherwise and enjoyed a 24-game unbeaten run.

United also had the biggest win of the season, a 7-1 home victory over Blackburn, although there were also 6-0 wins for Chelsea (v West Brom and Wigan), Arsenal (v Blackpool) and Newcastle (v Villa).

Chelsea hung on for the runner-up spot on goal difference as big-spending Manchester City reached third and a first time chance in the Champions League.

Brave Blackpool, back in the top-flight after a 39-year break and making their Premier League debuts, put on a good show but went straight back down.

Although it was very much a case of last-day drama with only West Ham certain to be relegated going into the final 90 minutes. Wolves and Wigan pulled off the great escapes as Birmingham City departed with Blackpool.

TOP SCORER

Dimitar Berbatov hit 20 league goals for Manchester United, the same number that Carlos Tevez scored for Manchester City. Tevez had 23 in all competitions to Berbatov's 21.

TOP TRANSFER

The biggest money transfer was the British record £50m move of Spain striker Fernando Torres from Liverpool to Chelsea. But the best buy was probably Man United's £6m purchase of Mexican striker Javier Hernandez from Guadalajara.

2010-11

THE ALL-TIME PREMIER LEAGUE TABLE

BARCLAYS PREMIER LEAGUE

Swansea became the 45th team to play in the Premier League when it kicked off in August 2011. Here are the points totals scored by the other 44 sides to appear in England's top-flight since the competition began in 1992-93. Everton and Newcastle will both be hoping to join the 1,000 points club during 2011-12.

#	Team	Points
1.	MAN UNITED	1,574
2.	ARSENAL	1,379
3.	CHELSEA	1,338
4.	LIVERPOOL	1,282
5.	ASTON VILLA	1,051
6.	TOTTENHAM	1,017
7.	EVERTON	978
8.	NEWCASTLE	952
9.	BLACKBURN	938
10.	WEST HAM	764
11.	MAN CITY	695
12.	LEEDS UNITED	692
13.	MIDDLESBROUGH	633
14.	SOUTHAMPTON	587
15.	BOLTON	539
16.	FULHAM	459
17.	COVENTRY	409
18.	SUNDERLAND	395
19.	SHEFF WED	392
20.	WIMBLEDON	391
21.	CHARLTON	361
22.	LEICESTER	339
23.	BIRMINGHAM	301
24.	PORTSMOUTH	293
25.	DERBY	274
26.	WIGAN	252
27.	NOTT'M FOREST	239
28.	IPSWICH	224
29.	QPR	216
30.	NORWICH	201
31.	WEST BROM	169
32.	CRYSTAL PALACE	160
33.	STOKE CITY	138
34.	SHEFFIELD UNITED	132
35.	WOLVES	111
36.	READING	91
37.	OLDHAM	89
38.	HULL	65
39.	BRADFORD CITY	62
40.	WATFORD	52
41.	BLACKPOOL	39
42.	BARNSLEY	35
43.	SWINDON	30
44.	BURNLEY	30

THE WORLD ACCORDING TO...
PATRICE EVRA

MANCHESTER UNITED'S FOUR-TIMES PREMIER LEAGUE WINNER

THE BIG MATCHES: "I like to win against Chelsea, I love to play against Manchester City and I hate to lose against Liverpool at Anfield. They are always our rivals. It is the worst pain you can have when you play for Manchester United. You need two or three days for recovery, there is silence and big disappointment in the dressing room."

PLAYING FOR UNITED: "Every young lad wants to play for us and respect the shirt. That's the only message you need to give. We know that when we play with spirit we can beat anyone. We need to win every game, we look to win the league. The priority is to make sure we win the league."

TEAM-MATE JI-SUNG PARK: "Ji's unbelievable. Sometimes when I am tired I know I'll be ok because Ji will run for me. I think he is one of the most important players in the team. He doesn't stop running, he can run all day. It must be the Korean food. Sometimes I go to his house and eat it!"

TOUGH TIMES: "When you have one bad game and people around you are criticising you, it makes you proud. In my first three years I had just one bad game, in the Carling Cup Final [2009] and the pitch was difficult – but I don't want to make excuses. I think criticism makes your stronger. Every year I think I have improved."

WAYNE ROONEY: "He has developed and understood that his job is to score goals. He channels his energies more and stays in the penalty area. He has increased responsibilities, particularly in attack. Sometimes it is down to him alone to decide matches for us but we are not dependent on Rooney."

TEAM SPIRIT: "When I am asked what team I fear most I always say United. It's not a question of being arrogant. I have a lot of respect for Chelsea, Arsenal, Liverpool and Villa but if we don't win the title every year we haven't done our job properly. The club is all about winning."

BAD TIMES: "When I was at Monaco in 2005 we were first in the league with ten games to go and we were playing Porto in the Champions League. We lost against Porto and we lost the league by one point. It was my worst-ever season."

HIS ARRIVAL AT UNITED IN 2006: "I got a load of DVDs, about the Munich disaster and the Busby Babes, about Bobby Charlton, George Best and Denis Law, about Cantona. You meet these people around the club and I wanted to know who they were. After I watched those DVDs I realised I needed to respect the shirt. I needed to respect the story."

FACT FILE

PATRICE LATYR EVRA
Position: Defender
Height: 1.73m (5ft 8in)
Birth Date: May 15, 1981
Birth Place: Dakar, Senegal
Clubs: Marsala, Monza, Nice, Monaco, Manchester United
International: France

DID YOU KNOW?

Evra believes his biggest honours include when he was named in the World's best XI [2009] and the Premier League XI three times [2007, 2009 2010]."

HIS DEAL TO 2014: "Ever since I arrived at United, it's been a dream come true playing here. I've won a lot in the last five years, but I want to win more and I know that's the mentality of everyone here."

SIR ALEX FERGUSON: "At 70, he doesn't see himself taking it easy at home reading a book or watching TV. Personally I think that would bore him. I don't think he will call an end to his career. As long as he's strong he will carry on. He will stay until his last breath."

ONES TO WATCH

10 PLAYERS EXPECTED TO BECOME MAJOR FORCES IN 2011-12

Every season a new batch of promising players realise their potential. Last campaign it was Gareth Bale and Jack Wilshere who made the grade and became major stars. Here are ten other young players set to go all the way to the top...

PHIL JONES

Club: Manchester United
Position: Central defender
Birth Date: February 21, 1992
Birth Place: Preston, Lancashire
International: England

An England Under-21 regular who impressed enough at Blackburn for Sir Alex Ferguson to cough up £16m to take him to Manchester United. Outstanding confidence and ambition for such a young player. Predicted to be a future captain for both club and country.

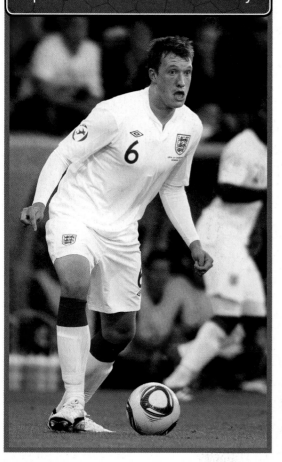

JOSH MCEACHRAN

Club: Chelsea
Position: Midfielder
Birth Date: March 1, 1993
Birth Place: Oxford
International: England

McEachran is the only English player since John Terry to come through the ranks at Chelsea. He is very highly rated by the management and his team-mates. Has a sweet left foot and a huge appetite for the game, plus the potential to be the next Frank Lampard.

RAHEEM STERLING

Club: Liverpool
Position: Striker
Birth Date: December 8, 1994
Birth Place: Kingston, Jamaica
International: England/Jamaica

Sterling has yet to nominate his international side, although he has appeared for England youth teams. The Liverpool schoolboy has got a big future ahead of him. Few youngsters have broken through at Anfield in recent years but this teenager is predicted to be a bit special.

HENRI LANSBURY

Club: Arsenal
Position: Midfielder
Birth Date:
October 12, 1990
Birth Place:
Enfield, North London
International: England

Who says Arsenal don't produce good English players? Lansbury has been on loan to Scunthorpe, Watford, Norwich and West Ham and made his mark at England Under-21 level. Made a big impact in Norwich's Championship promotion-winning side as an attacking midfielder.

KIERAN GIBBS

Club: Arsenal
Position: Left back
Birth Date: September 26, 1989
Birth Place: Lambeth, South London
International: England

With Gael Clichy departed to Man City, Gibbs will relish the chance to step straight into the Frenchman's boots. Already capped at senior level by England, he loves to get forward with pace and challenge opposition defenders. The Gunners probably won't realise the talented Clichy has been replaced!

CHRIS SMALLING

Club: Manchester United
Position: Central defender
Birth Date: November 22, 1989
Birth Place: Greenwich, South London
International: England

After just a handful of games at Fulham, following his arrival from non-League football, Sir Alex Ferguson had seen enough and coughed up £10m to take him to Man United. The England Under-21 star has improved further at Old Trafford in just one year. Set to be United's central defensive partnership with Phil Jones for years ahead. Often compared to Rio Ferdinand.

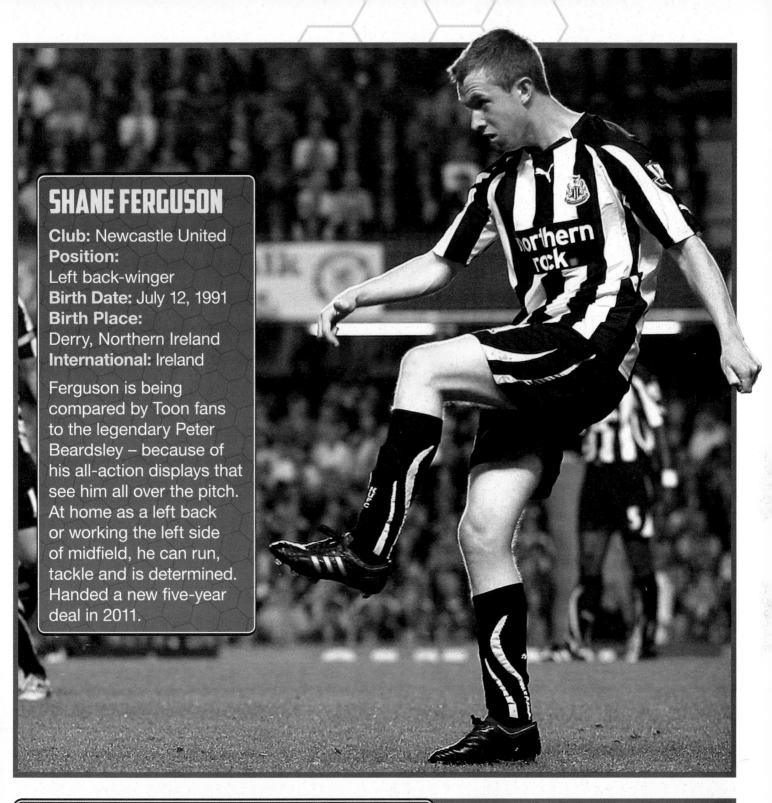

SHANE FERGUSON

Club: Newcastle United
Position:
Left back-winger
Birth Date: July 12, 1991
Birth Place:
Derry, Northern Ireland
International: Ireland

Ferguson is being compared by Toon fans to the legendary Peter Beardsley – because of his all-action displays that see him all over the pitch. At home as a left back or working the left side of midfield, he can run, tackle and is determined. Handed a new five-year deal in 2011.

JOSE BAXTER

Club: Everton
Position: Striker
Birth Date: February 7, 1992
Birth Place: Bootle, Merseyside
International: England

Everton have recently had a serious lack of goal-getters – but there is a view that teenager Baxter might well prove to be the next Wayne Rooney. Now the youngest-ever player to start a game for the Toffees, at 16 years and 191 days, he is at a crucial stage of his career.

NOW TURN THE PAGE FOR SPECIAL FEATURES ON TWO MORE PROMISING YOUNGSTERS...

GUNNER MAKE IT!

DANIEL BOATENG IS DETERMINED TO HIT ARSENAL HEIGHTS

Daniel Boateng has been rubbing shoulders with football aristocracy.

The Arsenal teenager has come up against Premier League strikers playing for the Gunners reserves and trained with Brazil when the Samba boys visited England!

AC Milan and Chelsea were reportedly looking at the player who can operate in defence or midfield – but Arsene Wenger handed the teenager a three-year contract last summer.

Now the defender plans to increase his number of reserve team games and push towards the Gunners' Premier League squad.

Shoot caught up with the quietly spoken but confident starlet after training…

How did you get into the game?
"A friend invited me to play for a local team, Broadwater, whilst I was at school. I did well there and Arsenal came and scouted me. It was a bit of a shock but I did play well that day."

Who were the players you looked up to?
"I was an Arsenal fan and at the time I thought Patrick Vieira was great. Although I am a central defender I can play at right back, left back, I can be quite versatile."

What about the current stars?
"I have to say the Chelsea captain John Terry is one of my favourites. Ledley King is great at the back and Ashley Cole is probably the greatest left back in the world and Micah Richards at right back."

What was it like leaving school and then training?
"To be honest there is no better thing. Academically at school I wasn't the best so to get paid for doing something I love so much is simply great."

Tell us a bit about what it's like?
"Pat Rice [Wenger's No.2] watches us train quite a bit and first-team coach Steve Bould also takes us at times. Liam Brady [head of youth development] called me in to tell me I would be getting a contract and I just thought 'all that hard work has paid off'."

So did many youngsters get released?
"I went to Arsenal at 11 and there were about 16 of us. Now there are only five. I've seen a lot of young players released and I knew it wouldn't be easy to get back into the game so I worked hard."

Has Arsene Wenger checked you out?
"Pat Rice is there all the time so he reports back to Mr Wenger and he knows how all of us are doing. My next step is to get more games for the reserves and probably to go out on loan and try to get into the Arsenal first-team."

Do you think a loan will help?
"There have been some good players who have gone out on loan from the club and not come back. So what I can say is that you have to keep working hard to get there."

A loan certainly helped Jack Wilshere!
"Jack is just one year older than me and when we went on tour he used to come with us so I have played with him quite a few times. There was also Jay Emmanuel-Thomas [now Ipswich] and Sanchez Watt [loan to Leeds]. All of those things have to give you a lot of hope."

Would you drop down leagues if you went out on loan?
"I know the main thing is to stay focused. I have heard that League One is good for defenders because of the kicking and tackling and as a defender that's what I have to learn how to cope with."

What are your strengths?
"I've got pace, I'm strong and I've got tricky feet. I'm becoming more of a leader too."

You're sounding like Arsenal legend Tony Adams!
[laughs] "…but I have got pace! He was one of the other players I really looked up to when I was playing as a kid."

So who have you faced in games so far?
"I played against Delfouneso [Aston Villa] and against Blackburn Rovers with Benjani and Jason Roberts. They were all very strong. At first I was nervous but as the games went on I thought I had to be good to even be on the same pitch as those players."

FACT FILE

DANIEL BOATENG
Position: Defender
Height: September 2, 1992
Birth Date: 1.83m (6ft)
Birth Place: London
Clubs: Arsenal

DID YOU KNOW?

Daniel could play for either Ghana or England – but he plans to keep his options open for now and see which international side will give him the best opportunity for making the most appearances.

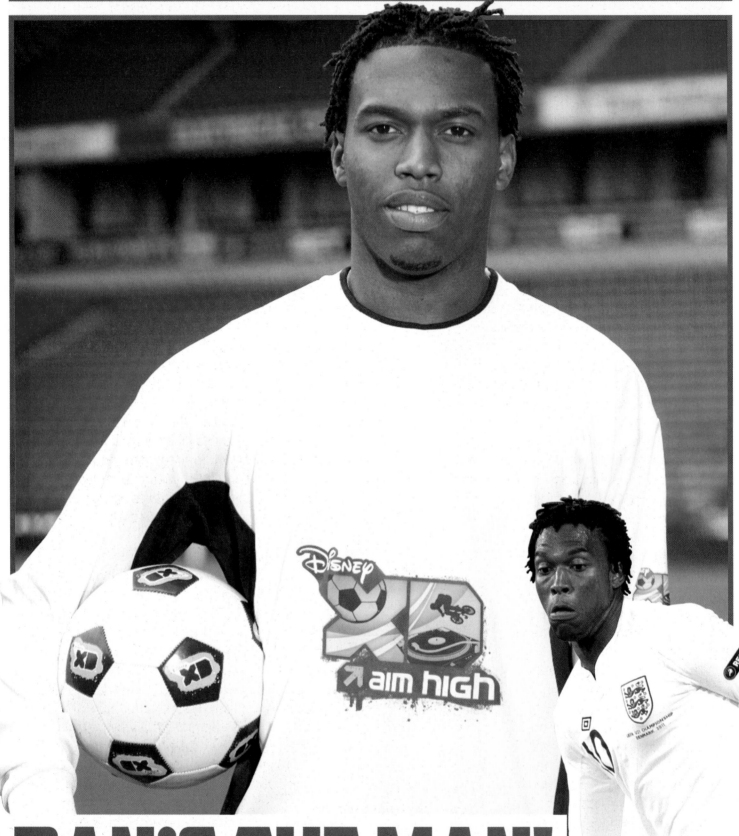

DAN'S THE MAN!

STRIKER STURRIDGE IS MAKING HIS MARK

When Daniel Sturridge made the move from Manchester City to Chelsea many pundits expected big things of him.

But his development at the Blues didn't happen quite like some expected with big names and big money signings keeping him out of the first-team.

On his rare appearances the young England striker showed very encouraging signs and boss Carlo Ancelotti was quick to sing his praises.

But all the time Sturridge knew that his game was developing and that a few regular appearances under his belt could kick start his career.

How right he was! A move to Bolton resulted in a rush of goals and performances that had fans raving.

"I wanted to go and play more regularly and the club gave me the chance to go on loan," Sturridge told *Shoot*.

"I spoke to Owen Coyle [Bolton manager] and it was a pretty easy decision to make. It went quite well – although some of the results could have gone better for us."

Went quite well was a bit of an understatement with four goals in his first five games for Wanderers in 2010-11. Confident Sturridge took it all in his stride: "Two goals straight off meant a lot to me. I have learned a lot watching great players like Didier [Drogba] and Nico [Nicolas Anelka] and other players in other positions because you have to learn their game too. I think I have learnt a lot since I went to Chelsea.

"I have learned a lot from two fantastic, great players and they have helped me to become who I am. I have taken stuff from their games and put it into mine.

"I looked on it as a great challenge having them in front of me – and I still think it is. But I have no doubts and no regrets about joining Chelsea, it is a great club."

The £50m arrival of Spain striker Fernando Torres might just have put a dampener on any young striker's hopes of breaking through, even though Drogba and Anelka are reaching the veteran stages of their career. But not for Sturridge...

"I was delighted Torres came in. The other two are not getting much younger, but they still have life in them and once they retire I will be there to take over from them."

INTERNATIONAL HOPES

Having proved himself at Bolton and made an impression at Chelsea, Sturridge has a whole list of ambitions he hopes to achieve during his football career.

"If I can play for the full England squad as well it will be a great achievement," he added.

"To represent my country at a World Cup would be a huge dream and to score as many goals in my career as I can is another aim.

"I watch England games and think it's a great bunch of players and hope that I will be able to get into the squad. Hopefully it can happen for me in the future."

He's taken the first step on the ladder to that dream having represented England at every level from Under-16 to Under-21s.

"It's great to represent my country at Under-21 level and would be amazing to step up to the full side in the future," said Sturridge.

"My parents have told me it is a great feeling when they see me in an England shirt. I don't know the emotion they are feeling but I am sure it is a good one and hopefully I can give it to them again if I play for the full international team. My England shirts are tucked away nicely at home!"

FAMILY AFFAIR

Older fans will hear the name Sturridge and instantly think of Dean – another striker, who played for a number of teams, including Derby, Wolves and QPR.

And it's no surprise to learn that Dean is Daniel's Uncle!

"He has played a big part, offered advice... and people call me Dean sometimes! I just let it slide like it never happened," smiled the youngster. "He has helped me a lot and so has my dad, Michael."

Dad Michael and another Uncle, Simon, were both on the books at Birmingham City. And cousin Chris played for Shrewsbury!

Uncle Dean rarely gets a chance to see Daniel play now as he works as a Sky Sports pundit but, like his dad, they are both at every game possible.

FACT FILE
DANIEL ANDRE STURRIDGE
Position: Striker
Height: September 1, 1989
Birth Date: 1.85m (6ft 1in)
Birth Place: Birmingham
Clubs: Manchester City, Chelsea, Bolton (loan)

DID YOU KNOW?
Daniel Sturridge had two big striking heroes when he was a youngster starting out. "Thierry Henry when he was at Arsenal and Ronaldo when he was at Barcelona. Those two are the ones I loved to watch. They had so much ability, so much talent and were also great to watch," he revealed.

TOTALLY TRUE!

SINGING STAR

When Ghana striker Asamoah Gyan isn't training or playing football you'll find him doing something musical.

The striker made a single called "African Girls" with singer Castro the Destroyer.

Gyan, who likes to be known as Baby Jet when singing, admits: "I like hip hop, Eminem, Sean Paul and listen to dancehall.

"I like any kind of music if the rhythm is good and I write my own songs. Everyone in the national team knows me and that I can sing morning to evening. I like to make people happy."

NET EFFECT

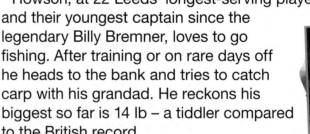

When Leeds midfielder Jonny Howson isn't on the pitch putting balls in the net – you'll find him by the waterside getting fish in his net!

Howson, at 22 Leeds' longest-serving player and their youngest captain since the legendary Billy Bremner, loves to go fishing. After training or on rare days off he heads to the bank and tries to catch carp with his grandad. He reckons his biggest so far is 14 lb – a tiddler compared to the British record.

IN TUNE FAN

Pop singer Adele reckons some would-be football fans are totally out of tune.

The voice of 'Hometown Glory' is Tottenham through and through and couldn't believe her luck when she found herself in the same hotel as the team.

Adele said: "I was born in Tottenham and have a shirt with Duchess 19 on the back. I almost called my dog Aaron Lennon because he's got little legs."

TOTTENHAM HOTSPUR

BOTTOM GEAR

Winger Jermaine Pennant is a fast worker on the pitch – but his memory works a little slower.

Pennant, who moved to Stoke City on a permanent deal from Real Zaragoza, forgot he had parked his super Porsche in Spain!

It had been left at the local railway station and when his former club contacted him he at first told them it wasn't his!

But the personalised number plate was a giveaway and Pennant had to get a pal to rescue the car and pay the fines. Mind you it might be easy to forget about the car when… you are already driving around England in a Ferrari!

FIXED PENALTY NOTICE

TWITTER KING

Rio Ferdinand is the king of Twitter with more than 1,300,000 followers.

The Manchester United and England defender reckons the on-line social network lets him keep in touch with fans and prove that he has his feet on the ground. Mind you, showing pictures of the meals he eats is a little bit much…

TUNED IN BOSS

Roberto Mancini is glad someone explained how to use the buttons on his TV remote – because it's helped him learn English.

The Manchester City boss had already taken a liking to Coronation Street but now he has discovered how to bring up subtitles the Italian reckons it has improved his knowledge of the local lingo.

"I have really enjoyed watching Coronation Street since I came to England," said the man dubbed Bobby Manc. "The subtitles have helped me to learn there are different accents so it has been educational as well."

·CORONATION ST.·

FOOTBALL'S FINEST

ROY KEANE

Nottingham Forest's relegation at the end of the first Premier League season saw Republic of Ireland midfield battler Keane transfer to Manchester United where he became a vital cog in their side and club captain.

He could be a midfield destroyer or creator but always had an influence on games. Became manager of Sunderland in 2006 and led them to promotion. Appointed boss of Ipswich in 2009 but sacked in January 2011. Made 366 PL appearances and scored 39 goals.

PREMIER LEAGUE YEARS
1992-05

GARY SPEED

The Wales midfielder played a staggering 535 Premier League games for Leeds United, Everton, Newcastle United and Bolton Wanderers.

Capped 85 times for his country, Speedo totalled more than 800 career appearances, rarely missing a game and nearly always putting in a reliable shift. Took over as manager of Sheffield United early in season 2010-11 before moving on to the Wales manger's job in December 2010.

PREMIER LEAGUE YEARS
1992-08

STAND UP AND APPLAUD SOME OF THE BEST PLAYERS EVER TO GRACE THE PREMIER LEAGUE. THESE GUYS HAVE NOW HUNG UP THEIR BOOTS BUT ANY TEAM WOULD LOVED TO HAVE HAD THEM IN THEIR SIDE!

DENNIS BERGKAMP

Twice Dutch footballer of the year, the first Holland star to be inducted into English football's Hall of Fame and voted by Arsenal fans as their Greatest Player ever.

Bergkamp played 316 PL games and scored 87 goals but his contribution as a midfielder-second striker was outstanding with killer passes and many assists. After retirement, moved back to his first team, Ajax, in a coaching role and also took on a similar job for Holland.

PREMIER LEAGUE YEARS
1995-06

ERIC CANTONA

Snapped up from champions Leeds United for just £1.2m at the start of the newly-formed Premier League, Cantona was the missing link in Sir Alex Ferguson's team.

Cantona helped United win the new division and set up the Red Devils for their domination of the Premier League. Often controversial – he was banned for kung-fu kicking a fan – he was also one of the most outrageously skilled players to appear in England. Made 156 PL appearances and scored 70 goals. Took over as director of football at New York Cosmos in January 2011.

PREMIER LEAGUE YEARS
1992-97

GOOD SPORTS!

Most footballers are sports mad! You will usually find they are a bit handy at sports other than football – and that members of their family are also a bit useful at games too. Here are a few of the sporting families…

OWENS

Michael Owen and dad Terry have played for the two big Merseyside rivals! Dad was on the books at Everton before joining Chester whilst Michael played for Liverpool before his moves to Real Madrid, Newcastle and Manchester United. Michael was also a bit handy at boxing as a youngster and has a very low golf handicap.

DAWSONS

Three Dawson brothers made it into League football – the youngest, Tottenham's Michael, reaching the senior England side. Michael joined Spurs from Nottingham Forest, where older brother Andrew and middle brother Kevin also began their careers.

STURRIDGES

England Under-21 striker Daniel Sturridge is the nephew of Dean Sturridge, who made his name as a hitman with Derby and Wolves. Uncle Simon, also a frontman, played for Birmingham and Stoke. Daniel's father, Michael, started at Birmingham City before going into non-league football.

JARVIS

When winger Matt Jarvis made his England debut in 2011 it was a massive thrill for the family. But mum Linda and dad Nick could already boast they had hit the heights at their own sport. They were both ranked as the country's No.1 at table tennis.

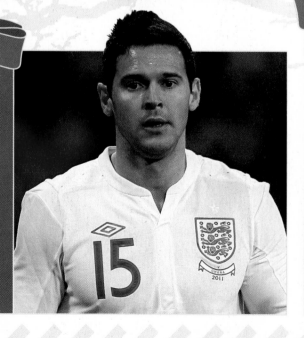

WRIGHTS

Dad Ian Wright not only played for England but also set a goal scoring record at Arsenal after making his name with Crystal Palace. Son Shaun Wright-Phillips has played for Manchester City and Chelsea as well as the national team. Younger brother Bradley has played for Man City, Southampton, Plymouth, Charlton and England Under-20s.

DALGLISH

Kenny Dalglish set high standards at football but son Paul still managed to follow him into the game and make a mark. After a career that took in a number of English clubs, including Newcastle, Norwich, Wigan and Blackpool, he went back to the Dalglish roots and played in Scotland. Paul then moved to America before venturing into management.

HUGHTONS

Chris Hughton was a respected defender with Spurs before earning praise as a coach at the club and then managing Newcastle to promotion from the Championship. His elder brother Henry was a star at Leyton Orient and Crystal Palace. Now, Chris' son Cian, who started at Tottenham, played last season with Lincoln City.

BRUCES

Steve Bruce made his name as a no-nonsense highly rated defender with Manchester United before moving into management with a number of clubs. Son Alex, a defender or midfielder, played under his father at Birmingham and a number of other sides before making a name at Ipswich and then with Leeds United.

FERDINANDS

Rio Ferdinand, former Man United and England captain, needs little introduction. His brother Anton has turned out for Sunderland and West Ham and cousin Les was a star striker with QPR, Newcastle and Spurs. Cousin Kane Ferdinand, a midfielder who made his name with Southend, has attracted interest from a number of clubs.

NEVILLES

The Neville family have a trio of England sports people in their ranks. Brothers Gary and Phil have both turned out for England at football whilst younger sister Tracey has played hockey for the Three Lions. Gary earned 85 caps, Phil 59 and Tracey 74.

HIGH CLIMBERS

It's a long way from the bottom to the top... but these guys have made it all the way up the footballing pyramid to the promised land of the Premier League!

CHRIS SMALLING

Chris Smalling now plays for the biggest team in England, is a regular for England Under-21s and on the verge of the senior squad.

But a few years ago it looked very unlikely he would make it as a professional footballer.

As a boy, he was signed by Millwall but only lasted two years before joining Maidstone at the tender age of 15. He quickly rose through the youth ranks and made his senior debut in 2007.

He played 11 games for the club before Middlesbrough attempted to sign him as the defender was trying to decide which University he should attend! Smalling chose Fulham instead, impressed by manager Roy Hodgson.

He made his Premier League debut for the Cottagers in 2009 and just a handful of games later Sir Alex Ferguson bought the player for £10m in January 2010.

United agreed Smalling could stay at Craven Cottage for the rest of the season.

Since arriving at Old Trafford he has quickly established himself as a member of the Manchester United first-team squad and is living up to his tag of "the new Rio Ferdinand" the player he is eventually expected to replace at the heart of United's defence.

JERMAINE BECKFORD

Jermaine Beckford is the former RAC patrolman who got his career on the road.

He began his career in the Chelsea youth team, where he teamed up with current England international Carlton Cole.

But he was released and joined Wealdstone in the Isthmian Premier League whilst he worked for the RAC.

Leeds United took the plunge in 2006 and signed him for £45,000 at the age of 22. Loans at Carlisle and Scunthorpe gained him experience before he returned to Elland Road and scored an impressive 72 goals in 126 appearances.

In May 2010, he signed for Everton in a £1m deal and move to Leicester for £2.5m in summer 2011.

GRANT HOLT

The part-time tyre fitter began his career with Barrow, Workington, Sengkang Marine in Singapore and Sheff Wed.

But a move to Rochdale in 2004 saw him score 42 goals in 83 games. Nottingham Forest then signed him for £300,000.

Holt failed to impress at the City Ground where he was used mostly as a winger. A move to Shrewsbury brought 28 goals in 51 games. That prompted Norwich City to sign him in 2009 and he helped them to League One promotion, being voted their Player of the Year with 30 goals in 44 games.

Holt scored 23 goals in 2010-11 to help Norwich return to the Premier League. He was again Player of the Season and short-listed for Championship Player of the Year.

KEVIN PHILLIPS

From factory shelf-stacker to a Premier League striker feared by defences, Kevin Phillips actually started his career as a right back!

Southampton released him as a youth player and he signed for non-league Baldock Town where he became a striker.

His goalscoring form attracted interest from a number of clubs, including Watford who signed Phillips for just £10,000 in 1994.

After two years at Vicarage Road he joined Sunderland, where he earned his Super Kev nickname.

There were goals galore from Phillips and he became the first player since Brian Clough to score 30 goals in a season for the Black Cats.

Phillips played 209 games for the club scoring 115 goals helping them gain promotion to the Premier League.

In 2003, when Sunderland were relegated, Southampton signed the player for £3.25m. He played for Aston Villa, West Brom and then Birmingham City, where he turned out in the top-flight in season 2010-11 at the age of 37. Joined Blackpool in summer 2011.

Phillips won the coveted European Golden Boot in 1999-00 with 30 goals for Sunderland.

MICHAEL KIGHTLY

Kightly was rejected as a schoolboy by Tottenham but shrugged off the disappointment and worked hard to earn a contract with Southend United.

A dozen appearances for the Seasiders and he was loaned out to Farnborough where his performances earned a move to Grays, and brought 24 goals in 53 league over two years.

Wolves signed him after a loan and in his first year he was runner in their Player of the Year award and helped them to a play-off spot.

Injury has hampered his progress but Sir Alex Ferguson once said the winger was regarded as the "Ryan Giggs of non-league football".

AND IT'S HAPPENED BEFORE...

From a day job to professional football and then onto international stardom...
here are some legends who really did rise from the bottom to the top!

STUART PEARCE

Famously worked as an electrician and played for Wealdstone before he joined Coventry City, Pearce even advertised his wiring services in the match day programme! Made his name as a tough, no-nonsense full back with Nottingham Forest and also played for Newcastle United, West Ham and Manchester City. Now England Under-21 boss and a coach with the seniors.

ENGLAND: 78 CAPS, 5 GOALS

CHRIS WADDLE

Before he became a feared winger, the lanky Geordie was a sweeper – with a brush in a factory that produced savoury products! Began his career with Newcastle United after leaving non-league Tow Law, then joined Spurs. Became a legend at Marseille where he won three French titles. Returned to England with Sheffield Wednesday. Now a TV pundit.

ENGLAND: 62 CAPS, 6 GOALS

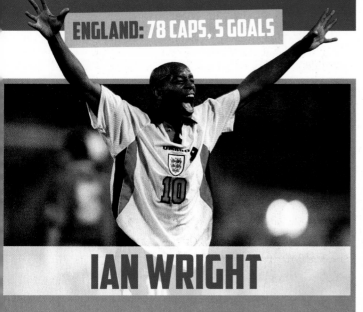

IAN WRIGHT

The striker was almost 22 when he was spotted playing for Dulwich Hamlet, having been rejected by Southend and Brighton. Transferred to Arsenal for £2.5m in 1991 and went on to become the Gunners' record goal scorer, as well as earning a Premier League medal and two FA Cups. Now a TV personality.

ENGLAND: 33 CAPS, 9 GOALS

LES FERDINAND

The painter and decorator joined QPR from non-league Hayes for £30,000 in 1987 and was sold to Newcastle eight years later for £6m! His departure is often blamed for Rangers slipping out of the top-flight. Scoring goals with power for his first two clubs, he was a popular frontman after joining Tottenham, where he is now a striker coach.

ENGLAND: 17 CAPS, 5 GOALS

WE ARE WINNERS

Picture highlights of some cracking results from 2010-11

BRILLIANT BARCA

Even Manchester United fans had to admit it – Barcelona were simply brilliant in the Champions League Final. It wasn't that United played badly, they were just overcome by the best side in the world. The planet's best player, Lionel Messi, helped to destroy them 3-1 with this goal, Barca's second.

SPOT-ON

Grant McCann watches the ball nestle in the bottom corner of the net after thumping it home from the penalty spot in his side's League One play-off semi-final victory against MK Dons. Posh then beat Huddersfield in the final.

HAT-TRICK HOT-SHOT

Scott Sinclair puts Swansea City on the road to a £90m windfall! This was his first, from the penalty spot, as he hit a hat-trick to help the Swans beat Reading 4-2 in the Championship play-off final. The win ensured that bumper payment as they became the first Welsh side in the Premier League.

CITY SLICKER

Yaya Toure smashes the FA Cup winner for Manchester City in the 1-0 victory against Stoke City. It earned his side their first trophy in 35 years.

LONG AND SHORT OF IT

Scorers Nikola Zigic (2.2m, 6ft 7.5in) and Obafemi Martins (1.7m, 5ft 7in) celebrate Birmingham City's 2-1 League Cup Final victory over Arsenal. It was the Blues first major trophy in 48 years.

Some 13 years ago Robbie Keane set off on an incredible international path to stardom.

That was the year he joined the Republic of Ireland senior ranks after a successful stay with their youth squads.

Now the striker has become the first UK and Ireland player to score more than 50 goals at international level – having already been the Republic's record goalscorer.

He is rated as the 12th best international scorer of all-time and ended 2010-11 as the Republic's third-highest appearance maker with 108 caps. That was just two appearances behind winger Kevin Kilbane and five behind keeper Shay Given.

Keane's 51 strikes for his country until the end of the last campaign put him 30 goals ahead of the previous record holder, Niall Quinn, who had 21.

QUINN DESERVES THE PRAISE

says Robbie Keane

" You can set your stall out to reach certain goals and my goal was to reach Niall Quinn's record [21]. When I first came into the Ireland squad Niall said to me I would get 50 goals, so it's probably down to him. As a kid you grow up dreaming of going out and playing for your country. You can ask any player in our squad, ask any player in any other country's squad. But I think the Irish players are more proud. I think I've proved over the years that I'm quite capable of doing a job and scoring goals. I know that for a fact that as long as I am given an opportunity I will score goals. As long as I am playing I am happy but I can't score if I'm not on the pitch. There is a difference between physical and match fitness. I am a player who likes to play all of the time and I get my fitness and sharpness from that. "

SHOOT TRIBUTE

ROBBIE'S RECORD

KEANE'S THE UK AND IRELAND GOAL KING

WHAT THEY SAY...

"I am delighted for Robbie. He is a special talent and deserves to have scored as many as he has. Hopefully he will carry on scoring more goals for his country."

Giovanni Trapattoni
Republic of Ireland boss

"He's been an amazing striker for Ireland. He's going to set a target that I don't think anyone will ever reach and he's got plenty more years left in him yet."

John O'Shea
Republic team-mate

"Robbie is phenomenal and it's a phenomenal record – he deserves all the headlines and all the credit because it's fantastic. It's not just for his goals, but his leadership as a captain."

Shay Given Ireland's
record-appearance holder

"Only a few players have got Robbie's enthusiasm. When he loses the ball he chases after it like kids do in the playground. He's got that little bit of class you are looking for. He has great enthusiasm for the game, he loves playing. He's a fantastic professional footballer." **Harry Redknapp** Tottenham manager

FACT FILE
ROBERT DAVID KEANE
Position: Striker
Birth place: Dublin
Birth date: July 8, 1980
Height: 1.75m (5ft 9in)
Clubs: Wolves, Coventry, Inter Milan, Leeds, Spurs (2), Liverpool, Celtic (loan), West Ham (loan), LA Galaxy
Ireland debut: 1998, 2-0 friendly defeat to Argentina in Dublin.
First goal for Ireland: v Malta, October 1998

DID YOU KNOW?
● Robbie was appointed Ireland captain in 2006, two years after becoming the Republic of Ireland's record scorer.
● His first 100 games for the Republic yielded 43 goals.
● Inter Milan bought Robbie in 2000 for £13m – a transfer fee that means he cost them £1m for every game in which he played!
● After seeing pictures taken by *Shoot* for the magazine he asked for copies for his mum's house.
● In celebration of Robbie's record, the Republic launched a commemorative Umbro shirt celebrating his 50 goals.

KEY YEARS
1997 Made debut for Wolves at the age of 17.

1999 Joined Coventry City for one season.

2000 Moved to Inter Milan.

2001 Joined Leeds United on loan before making the move permanent.

2002 Signed for Tottenham for £7m

2008 Robbie moved to Liverpool. Six months later he was back at Tottenham.

2010 Went on loan to Celtic and reached the 100 game mark for the Republic.

2011 Loaned to West Ham for the second half of the season. Reached 50 goals mark for the Republic. Joined LA Galaxy for £3.5m

ATTACK, ATTACK, ATTACK!

WHEN SUPPORTERS SHOUT 'ATTACK' TEAMS KNOW WHAT TO DO. BUT WHEN PLAYERS AND FANS LAUNCH INTO BATTLE ANYTHING CAN HAPPEN! THESE ARE SOME OF FOOTBALL'S WORST ATTACKING INCIDENTS!

BRING THEM ON!

Roy Keane wasn't called a battling midfielder for nothing – he took on all-comers during his time at Manchester United!

The Republic of Ireland star had a bust up in the tunnel with fellow captain Patrick Vieira of Arsenal and earned himself a red card for decking Newcastle skipper Alan Shearer. Keano also saw red for elbowing Jason McAteer of Sunderland and for stamping on Gareth Southgate, of Crystal Palace.

Keane also admitted that he had gone for payback on Alf Inge Haaland, then of Leeds, four years after the Irishman had been injured himself during a tackle on the Norway star. Keane put his right boot into Haaland's knee to end his season – and effectively his career – and was fined £150,000. Haaland was then playing for Manchester City.

KING CLOUGH

Legendary boss Brian Clough always said what he thought – and that's why supporters loved him so much.

Three so-called football fans, who were part of a pitch invasion, discovered that Cloughie wasn't a man to be messed with!

After his Nottingham Forest side won against QPR, Clough was not amused to see fans on the pitch so he lashed out at the three, punching one of them.

No charges were brought although Cloughie had to sit in the stands for the rest of the season.

TOUGH JOB!

Local rivalry doesn't come much stronger than in Glasgow where Rangers and Celtic both play their games.

And Celtic boss Neil Lennon knows more than most what it's all about having received death threats, a bullet and parcel bombs in the post! He also had to dodge a flying fist when a fan ran at him during a game with Hearts.

CRIME DOESN'T PAY

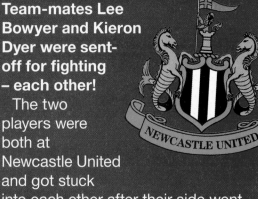

You should know better than mess with a 1.93m (6ft 4in) tall Scotsman with a reputation as a hard man who had been in jail for assaulting a player during a game!

Two burglars obviously didn't rate Everton and Scotland striker Duncan Ferguson as highly as his reputation – but came off worst! One escaped – only to be caught later – whilst the other was pinned to the ground by Big Dunc until the police arrived. The burglar who was caught spent a few days in hospital.

AND THEY WERE MATES...

Team-mates Lee Bowyer and Kieron Dyer were sent-off for fighting – each other!

The two players were both at Newcastle United and got stuck into each other after their side went 3-0 down to Aston Villa. Bowyer's shirt was ripped and the pair were sent off in front of bemused fans.

UNITED FRONT!

Eccentric Frenchman Eric Cantona hit the headlines when he launched a kung-fu kick at a Crystal Palace fan after being sent off at Selhurst Park.

The Manchester United legend was banned for four months and fined £30,000 but later said it was a highlight of his career!

"When I did the kung-fu kick on the hooligan, because these kind of people don't have to be at the game," said the forward.

"I think maybe it's like a dream for some, you know sometimes to kick these kind of people."

Meanwhile, his United team-mate Gary Neville was sent off in a defeat against Everton for kicking the ball into the crowd.

Ironically, the ball hit a Red Devils' fan who was one of Neville's biggest admirers!

KOREA MOVERS

The arrival of striker Ji Dong-Won at Sunderland took the number of South Koreans to play in the Premier league to eight. Dong-Won, just 20, is one of the hottest properties on the planet, a tag that has also been handed to some of his fellow countrymen, but not always with justification...

THE HITS

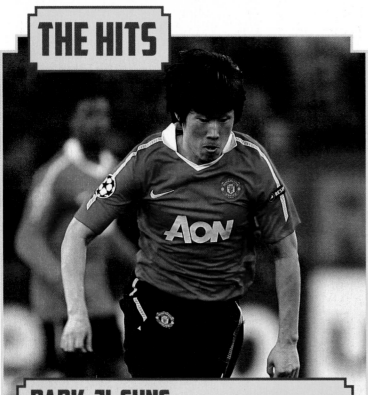

PARK JI-SUNG
MANCHESTER UNITED 2005-PRESENT

The first and by far the best of his countrymen to play in the English top-flight, Park has well and truly buried suggestions that he was bought to sell more shirts!

The critics pounced when he arrived at Old Trafford from PSV Eindhoven for £4m, despite having a big reputation in Holland.

The accusation was that United had bought the player to increase their appeal in Asia and sell a stack of replica shirts. They may have sold more shirts but it is on the strength of the player's ability rather than the loyalty of his fellow countrymen.

Park, now 30, has been a key member of Sir Alex Ferguson's squad and a player for the big, demanding occasions. Has four Premier League winners' medals, three League Cups and a Champions League to his name with United.

LEE CHUNG-YONG
BOLTON, 2009-PRESENT

The 24-year-old winger has earned rave reviews during his two years at the Reebok Stadium and has even been linked with a move to Liverpool.

Lee cost just £2.2m from FC Seoul and his first campaign earned Bolton's Player of the Year and Players' Player of the Year awards.

He's learnt English during his time with Bolton and appeared for his country at World Cup 2010.

LEE YOUNG-PYO
TOTTENHAM, 2005-08

The left-back earned a lot of respect at White Hart Lane following his move from PSV Eindhoven where he had twice won the Dutch League plus Holland's FA Cup.

Signed by former boss Martin Jol, Lee was a no-nonsense defender who played 93 games and won the League Cup before leaving for Borussia Dortmund.

Has since played in Saudi Arabia for Al Hilal but at the age of 34 is considering retirement before the new season gets under way.

SEOL KI-HYEON
READING AND FULHAM, 2006-10

Had played in the Championship with Wolves for two years before a season in the Premier League with Reading and then a spell with Fulham.

Now 32, and back playing in Korea, Seol cost the Royals £1.5m and scored four goals in 30 league games. His time at the Madejski Stadium, where the fans sang his name, came to an end as he didn't see eye to eye with boss Steve Coppell.

Seol agreed a three-year deal with Fulham in summer 2007 but, unable to earn a regular spot at Craven Cottage, he went out on loan before the club agreed to terminate his contract.

THE MISSES

KIM DO-HEON
WEST BROM 2008-09

Nicknamed the "Asian Paul Scholes", Kim never really lived up to anywhere near those expectations!

He played four games on loan from Seongnam Ilhwa Chunma and scored a goal to help the Baggies earn promotion to the Premier League and himself a permanent move for £500,000.

But just 12 months, 19 games and two goals later he was on his way home for £360,000. Now 29, he is still turning out for his country.

LEE DONG-GOOK
MIDDLESBROUGH 2006-08

After 29 games and just two goals – one in the FA Cup and one in the League Cup – Gook was a gonner from the Riverside!

Other than seven games with Werder Bremen in Germany he had never played outside of Korea until his move to England.

His contract was not renewed when it expired. Now 32 and back in South Korea. Was part of their 2010 World Cup squad and top scorer in the K-League two years ago.

CHO WON-HEE
WIGAN, 2009-11

A host of top European clubs had chased the midfielder's signature but the free agent plumped for Wigan – where he made the grand total of five appearances, four of those as a sub. He was loaned out for a year before being given a free to Chinese Super League side Guangzhou Evergrand last February.

20 QUESTIONS

TO TEST YOUR FOOTBALL KNOWLEDGE

KNOW IT ALL WHEN IT COMES TO FOOTBALL? THINK YOU ARE SMARTER THAN JOHN MOTSON OR MARTIN TYLER? WELL HERE IS YOUR CHANCE TO PROVE IT! OR AT LEAST TRY!

Q1

Who scored the first-ever goal in the Premier League?

A. Alan Shearer

B. Brian Deane

C. Ryan Giggs

Q2

Nigel Clough is the son of legendary Forest boss Brian. Which club did Clough jnr manage before Derby?

A. Burton Albion   B. Notts County
C. Brentford

Q3

In which country was Arsene Wenger managing before he took over as Arsenal boss?

A. France
B. Japan
C. Italy

Q4

Kenny Dalglish is back as boss of Liverpool. How many times did he play for the Reds?

A. 422   B. 515   C. 611

Q5

Who is England's most-capped player?

A. David Beckham
B. Peter Shilton
C. Bobby Moore

Q6

Who scored the winning goal for Spain in the 2010 World Cup Final?

A. Fernando Torres
B. Andres Iniesta
C. David Villa

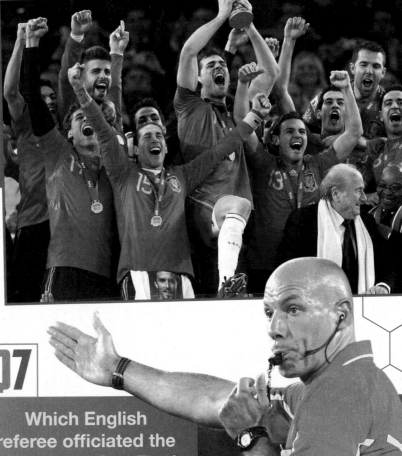

Q7

Which English referee officiated the 2010 World Cup Final in South Africa?

A. Chris Foy
B. Mike Dean
C. Howard Webb

Q8

Former Newcastle and England captain Alan Shearer is the Premier League's record goalscorer. How many did he hit?

A. 190   B. 260
C. 301

Q9

Juliano Belletti played in the Premier League for Chelsea. But which country did he turn out for?

A. Brazil   B. Argentina
C. Italy

Q10

At the end of season 2010-11, how many Premier League winner's medals had Ryan Giggs picked up?

A. 10   B. 11   C. 12

Q11

Name the odd one out – and why?

A. Joe Cole
B. Scott Parker
C. Frank Lampard

Q12

England have the oldest Football Association in the world – which country has the second-oldest?

A. Scotland   B. China   C. Wales

The FA

Q13

Which of these players had won the most Republic of Ireland caps until the end of season 2010-11?

A. Niall Quinn
B. Robbie Keane
C. Shay Given

Q14

England keeper Joe Hart started his career at his home town club. Which team was it?

A. Blackpool
B. Shrewsbury
C. Birmingham

Q15

Who is the odd one out – and why?

A. David Beckham   B. Michael Owen   C. Gary Neville

Q16

Which of these three was the youngest when he turned out for England?

A. Jack Wilshere
B. Wayne Rooney
C. Theo Walcott

Q17

Edwin van der Sar announced his retirement from Manchester United in 2011. Which Italian side did he also play for?

A. Juventus   B. Roma   C. AC Milan

Q18

The most number of people to attend a British league match...

A. 96,071   B. 101,922   C. 118,567

Q19

Who was England's oldest-ever player?

A. Teddy Sheringham
B. Stanley Matthews
C. Peter Shilton

Q20

Who is Wales' record goalscorer?

A. Craig Bellamy
B. Ian Rush
C. Dean Saunders

ANSWERS

Q1. B	Q11. B
Q2. A	Q12. A
Q3. B	Q13. C
Q4. B	Q14. B
Q5. B	Q15. C
Q6. B	Q16. C
Q7. C	Q17. A
Q8. B	Q18. C
Q9. A	Q19. B
Q10. C	Q20. B

Question 11
All have played for
West Ham and Chelsea,
but Cole and Lampard
began their careers
with the Hammers.

Question 15
The other two wore
the No.7 shirt

Question 18
Rangers v Celtic 1939